The Glory of
GREECE
and the World of Alexander

The Glory of
GREECE
and the World of Alexander

by Michael Davison

Introduction by
DR. ALAN W. JOHNSTON

Department of Classical Archaeology,
University College, London

ABBEVILLE PRESS • PUBLISHERS • NEW YORK

FRONT COVER
Alexander as Demigod
TITLE PAGE
A King of the Earliest Greeks
Commentaries on page 172

Photo credits:
Front cover and pages 125, 135: Courtesy of the
Trustees of the British Museum. Title page and
pages 49, 89, and 153: Ronald Sheridan. Pages 129-131:
David Finn. Page 133: EPA/Scala. All other photo-
graphs: Michael Holford Library.

Library of Congress Cataloging in Publication Data
Main entry under title:

The Glory of Greece and The World of Alexander.

    Bibliography: p. 168
    1. Art, Greek.   2. Greece—Antiquities.
I. Davison, Michael.
N5630.G55   709′.38   79-92450
ISBN 0-89659-104-2

Book Design: Roy Winkler

Contents

Introduction

Greek speakers first entered the Balkan peninsula some four thousand years ago. Fifteen hundred years later they were present in many part of the Mediterranean seaboard, from Spain to the Nile Delta and into the Black Sea. By 323 B.C. Alexander had taken the Greek way of life into Afghanistan and beyond, to Pakistan and the Punjab. Soon after his death the borders of this Greek world began to crumble once more, but its artistic and literary influence remained strong, especially in that new imperial power, Rome.

The path from 2000 to 323 B.C. was not a smooth one of gradual progress and improvement. The baronial rulers of Mycenae had built up an efficient and organized civilization by 1500 B.C., borrowing generously in their artistic output from the non-Greek Minoans of Crete. Their rule flourished for over three hundred years, no doubt with many local feuds and fluctuations, until a series of destructions shattered their central organization and put an end to the extravagancies of life for the long period extending from 1150 to after 800 B.C.—the Greek Dark Ages. The cause of this decline is disputed: famine, invasion, civil conflict—perhaps all three. One of the techniques lost was that of writing. The Mycenaeans had earlier adapted a Minoan syllabic script for the needs of their accountants, but it was not until 750 B.C. that Greek was once more written down, this time in an alphabet borrowed from the Phoenicians of the eastern Mediterranean. One addition made by the Greek transcriber of this alphabet was of special significance: the vowels, without which the direct successors of the Phoenicians still write.

The slow increase in standards of living during these centuries is clear in the archaeological records.

Slowly, more elaborate and monumental dwellings and artifacts emerged; slowly the Greek world expanded once more to regain contact with neighbors to west and east, and it was from the east that much more than the alphabet was borrowed. Ideas of all kinds, from the working of hard stone to cosmologies, were absorbed and more often than not transmuted by Greeks in many of the small feudal states of the mainland. Monumentality became a proof of status, whether in the size of the jar set above one's parent's grave or the statue dedicated in the most important sacred sanctuary of a town. Artists too began to advertise themselves; the earliest signed works we have are vases and sculptures of the seventh century B.C.

Much of the subject matter of these artists had its roots in the Near East, in Phoenician metalwork and Syrian ivories, and probably textiles as well. But in Greece the hieratic and symbolic meaning of much of these borrowings was ignored, and a fresh art emerged based on linear clarity and carefully balanced masses, whether in vase-painting or the plastic arts. Decorated vases are a prime source of our knowledge of Greek mythology and many aspects of everyday life; they are also a yardstick of artistic taste and development and they enable us to date our archaeological strata with enviable precision. This is because in the hands of its better practitioners Greek art was never static; development of detail and composition was constant, and in vase-painting this applied as much to techique as to draftsmanship. To our eye the figures on vases of the eighth century B.C. are childish matchstick men and animals. Gradually, with the use of outline drawing, and in particular the incision of detail with a point in the dark surface, they become more animated. This "black-figure" technique was inhibitive, however, since the incised line was the only method of showing inner detail. Still, the technique was popular in many areas; tens of thousands of black-figure vases were exported from Athens in the sixth and early fifth centuries. In the latter part of the sixth century B.C. came a change in vase-painting technique, with a reversal of the roles of dark and light areas; in "red-figure" work, painted lines supplied the detail and could be used with greater freedom and variety than incision. A growing interest in anatomy and pose is reflected in all the arts during the sixth and fifth centuries, but particularly in vase-painting and sculpture; had more than the merest snatch of free painting survived, we would no doubt see the same trends there. Such an interest in the improvement of detail was only one expression of Greek curiosity—the same inquisitiveness was, for example, to give rise to our earliest scientific philosophy among the Greeks of Asia Minor.

In sculpture, the types of free-standing monument were few in the early years; most were standing figures in a hieratic stance borrowed from Egypt. Yet a new material was used—native Greek marble—and the sculptors broke away from Egyptian rigidity by constantly attempting to impart individuality. One feature of Greek sculpture and architecture that is too often forgotten is the free use of paint—red, blue, green, gold. Many of the statues that were smashed by the Persians when they took Athens in 480 and buried by the returning exiles the next year still retain much of their color, and even on marbles long exposed to the elements the ghosts of painted patterns can still be made out.

So a Greek temple with its sculpted pediments and gargoyles was a much more colorful object than now appears. In architectural sculpture there were more opportunities to experiment with complex groupings and action, despite the severe limitations of the low triangle of the pediment. Such a low-pitched roof was needed because the tiles were held in place by gravity alone—one of the many practical considerations that gave rise to the developed temple design, a far cry from the small mud-brick cabins with thatched roof in which the cult statues of the Dark Ages were kept. As in many other fields of life, rivalry among individuals, families, and states was undoubtedly a powerful force in the increasing scale and sophistication of temple design. Temples of neighboring states in both Asia Minor and Sicily were clearly rivals for the record book. At Olympia in the 460s, Zeus was honored with a mathematically proportioned large temple; later, Phidias constructed for it the enormous seated cult figure in gold and ivory, though in the meantime he had ensured that the Parthenon at Athens was built on an even grander scale to house his other gold and ivory masterpiece, the 39-foot-high Athena.

Many of these structures are now shattered shells, but by way of compensation we have preserved countless smaller artifacts of the period—vases, bronzes, gems, coins, and the often humble terra-cotta figurine. All reflect the passage from the straightforward, often gaudy expressiveness of the seventh and sixth centuries B.C. to the restrained emotions and noble features of the classical style of the fifth. It is a curious progression, which probably owed as much to the influence of the techniques of large-scale bronze statuary and the limpid deities of Phidias as to a general panhellenic tendency towards greater introspectiveness and self-examination. Indeed, the bland expressions all too often belong to figures in violent action, or posed so as to display the virtuoso effects of the modelling of drapery or muscular masses—tendencies of ever more concern to the practitioners of the plastic arts in the ensuing centuries.

Throughout, artists and artisans were dependent for their livelihood on patronage and trade; in the average-sized Greek "city-state" of about two thousand souls, few men could be so supported. In addition, an economy based on coinage did not emerge until the later fifth century. As a result, stylistic centers of art were few, and until the later sixth century they were to a greater or lesser extent independent of each other. Athens was one of the largest Greek states, along with Sparta (with her subject serf population), Argos, Corinth, Samos, and Miletus; it was in such areas that the greatest artistic impulses were created. Ancient authors mention leading painters from Athens and the Peloponnese, but we see only their reflection in other works—vases, mosaics, and later Roman copies; much the same applies to the famous classical sculptors, Polyclitus of Argos, Phidias, and Praxiteles of Athens. Their originals were long since melted down for swords—or ploughshares.

Much precious metal too was melted down in the

10

course of the great Peloponnesian war of 431-405 B.C., when the Athenian coffers were drained in the vain effort to sustain her control over the Aegean. Athens' recovery was slow in the fourth century, and the initiative passed to other mainland states, especially in the Peloponnese. Mercenaries played an increasing role in warfare. Improved siege techniques during this period resulted in some of the best preserved Greek fortification walls, as well as civic buildings of less martial character, especially theaters. (It is ironic that the great tragedians of the fifth century put on their works in far less luxuriously appointed surroundings.) At the same time the significance of the individuals within the state increased, leading not only to greater sophistication in private housing, but also to the rise of what we may truly call portrait sculpture.

These trends continue apace after Madecon became the dominant power in Greece and the rest of the Near and Middle East, during the reigns of Philip and his son Alexander. Their military success was based on the income from the rich mines of Pangaios, east of Thessalonike, and then the captured treasury of the Persian king. Dispute over the succession to Alexander, who died in Babylon at the age of 32, led to a series of conflicts between his successors, the Diadochi—Ptolemy in Egypt, Lysimachus and Seleucus in the Near East, and Antigonus and Demetrius in Greece; yet at the same time city life began to flourish once more, especially in Asia Minor and in the many cities named Alexandria by their founder. The Greeks in Sicily also experienced a revival in fortunes after bloody civil wars. This was the basis of much exciting work in architecture and sculpture in the third and second centuries B.C. It was partly deeply rooted in the classical style, partly sentimentally ornate, and partly monumentally exhibitionist, ranging from the whimsical terra-cotta figurines from Tanagra and Myrina to portraits of heroic Olympic victors or deified rulers and expansively planned civic centers with marbled halls. It was such Hellenistic munificence that inspired the art and architecture of imperial Rome.

—A.W.J.

11

LION GATE AT MYCENAE

The ruins of the fortified city of Mycenae, in southern
Greece, still stand as an impressive memorial to the
achievements of the Mycenaean civilization between
1500 and 1150 B.C. Mycenae became the most
powerful among a number of warlike kingdoms
scattered throughout Greece, ruled by kings living in
splendor in heavily defended fortress cities.

This great Lion Gate at Mycenae foreshadows the
triumphs of Greek architecture in later years in its
combination of function and grandeur. To lessen the
weight pressing on the lintel of the gateway, the
massive stone blocks of the city walls are broken by a
lighter, triangular slab of gray stone, which is
decorated with two finely carved heraldic lions.

The power of the Bronze Age Mycenaeans crumbled
when the less-civilized Dorians moved into Greece
from the north. The Mycenaean strongholds decayed
and Greece entered a "Dark Age," which was to
last for three centuries until civilization revived. But
the exploits of the Mycenaeans were not forgotten,
and they formed the basis for the epic stories of
Greece's heroic age that were narrated by Homer
and his contemporaries around 700 B.C. According to
the historian Thucydides, it was the Mycenaeans'
struggle to keep open their trade route to the Black
Sea that sparked off the Trojan War—though legend
was later to attribute the war to a more romantic cause.

c. 1250 B.C.

CARVING IN IVORY

The wealth of the Bronze Age Mycenaean civilization in Greece was largely founded on widespread trade throughout the Aegean world. The Mycenaeans imported textiles, gold, ivory, and spices, and exported oil, perfume, and ivory carvings. A wide variety of Mycenaean products have been found as far afield as Sicily and Tarentum in the west and Syria and Egypt in the east.

This ivory box was found in a tomb at Enkomi, in eastern Cyprus. The technique of ivory carving came, with the ivory itself, from the east, and this design of two bulls by an unknown Mycenaean craftsman may be an echo of the even earlier civilization of the Minoans in Crete, whose work strongly influenced the Mycenaeans. The bull was greatly revered by the Minoans, and may have symbolized the power of the earthquakes that often shook Crete.

In the wake of the traders, colonists from mainland Greece settled on Aegean islands and on the west coast of Asia Minor. Cyprus was a popular destination, and from 1200 B.C. onward, the new settlers began making vases and other typical Mycenaean wares on the island.

c. 1300 B.C. British Museum, London

WINE JUG WITH GEOMETRIC DESIGN

Clay was the raw material for a wide range of Greek household objects, from lamps and cooking pots to children's toys. The potter was an important craftsman, producing large quantities of pots in various shapes and sizes to hold olive oil, water, wine, and corn. Since the potter or his colleagues decorated the clay vases, the potter's workshop was also something of an artist's studio.

At first the principal form of decoration was based on straight-line patterns; this artistic era, known as the Geometric period, roughly spans the ninth and eighth centuries B.C. The entire surface of this *oinochoe*—a one-handled jug used for serving wine—is covered with geometric designs. The characteristic meander, or "Greek key," pattern forms the largest motif, surrounded by zigzags and triangles. Continuous diamond-pattern friezes encircle the vase at salient points to emphasize its shape. The patterned zones are divided from each other by firm triple lines.

Earthenware pots found in graves furnish most of our knowledge of Greek art after the Dark Age, when civilization was reviving in Greece in numerous independent city-states. Other artifacts of the time have perished; but clay pots, buried in the ground, have survived the passage of the centuries. Often they are found in shattered fragments, which have been painstakingly pieced together to testify to the combined skills of the artist and potter of 2,700 years ago.

c. 750 B.C. British Museum, London

WARRIORS OF EARLY GREECE

The geometric patterns of early vase decoration soon began to be supplemented with renditions of men and animals. The figures in this vase painting are recognizably human warriors, carrying swords and spears. They are drawn in a stylized manner, however, to form an abstract shield motif, and arranged in an ornamental frieze that harmonizes with the geometric meander band beneath them.

The decoration was painted on by brush, using a shiny brown glaze of liquid clay. The glaze darkened during firing, leaving the painted areas standing out against the light background of the vase. This particular jar, probably a funeral vase made for a tomb, comes from Attica, the area around Athens which in the eighth century B.C. was one of the most important of Greece's city-states and a major artistic center.

The stylization of the human figure gradually gave way to a more realistic treatment, foreshadowing the skillful realism of later Greek artists and sculptors. However, the love of symmetry inherited from the artists of the Geometric period remained a guiding influence on Greek art, and was reflected in the balance and harmony sought by the finest Classical artists, architects, and sculptors.

c. 730 B.C. British Museum, London

CENTAUR ON A GOLD PLAQUE

Greek craftsmen showed exceptional skill at molding intricate jewelry from gold and silver. This embossed gold plaque, just over one and a half inches high, is one of a string of similar pieces, which were worn across the breast like a low necklace. It was found in a grave at Camirus on the island of Rhodes, the center of a prosperous Greek trading settlement with fine goldsmiths' workshops in the mid-seventh century B.C.

Large quantities of gold, silver, and ivory were brought to Greece and the Greek islands by traders from the Near East and Asia Minor. These merchants also brought back ornaments decorated with oriental and Egyptian motifs, and these encouraged Greek artists to add animal and human figures to their early geometric patterns. The hairstyle of the Centaur on this plaque is recognizably eastern in inspiration. The mythical character is shown here with the barrel and hindquarters of a horse attached to a complete human body; in later Greek art, the human part of the Centaur was reduced to the head and torso alone, with the lower body and four legs those of a horse. The Centaurs were usually portrayed in Greek myth as a barbarian race, enemies of civilized society; but one benign Centaur, Chiron, was renowned for his wisdom and was regarded as the teacher of such heroes as Jason and Achilles.

Seventh century B.C. British Museum, London

TEMPLE OF APOLLO AT CORINTH

For centuries these Doric columns of a ruined Temple of Apollo, on a headland overlooking the sea, were the only relics of the ancient city of Corinth. Excavations in modern times have revealed further remains of one of the most powerful and wealthy city-states of ancient Greece.

Around 800 B.C., civilization began to revive in Greece following a 300-year Dark Age. The new civilization developed in a number of small, separate city-states often built around a hilltop citadel within which its citizens could defend themselves from attack. Corinth's citadel was the craggy 1,500-foot Acrocorinth. Below the northern slopes of the hill eventually grew up a city enclosed by a ten-mile wall and containing temples, fountains, a theater, and a large racetrack. The Temple of Apollo is an early example of the Doric order; originally it had thirty-eight columns—fifteen along each side and six across each end.

Corinth owed its early importance among Greek city-states to its strategic position on an isthmus between two seas—the Aegean Sea and the Gulf of Corinth. From Corinth, colonists sailed westward to Italy and Sicily, and fabrics and ivories imported from the East influenced Corinthian potters to introduce floral patterns and human and animal figures to their own work. The city grew wealthy by exporting oil, wine, and decorated pottery all over the Mediterranean world. But by the mid-sixth century B.C., the potters of Athens, with access to better-quality clay, eclipsed the Corinthian artisans. In 146 B.C., Corinth was sacked by the Romans; a century later, however, Julius Caesar rebuilt it as the capital of his Roman province of Achaia.

c. 560-550 B.C.

LION JUG FROM RHODES

The art of the potters of Corinth, whose products reached every corner of the Greek world, is typified by this fine decorated wine jug, found in a cemetery at Camirus in Rhodes. The island of Rhodes was colonized as early as Mycenaean times, and with the revival of civilization in mainland Greece by the eighth century B.C., the Rhodian settlers prospered through trade with the emergent Greek city-states.

The geometric designs of the earliest Corinthian vases were soon supplemented by floral patterns and figures of animals and humans, based on the motifs of bronzes and ivories imported from the Near East and from Asia Minor; the figures retained their Corinthian flavor, however, by virtue of their arrangement in a symmetrical pattern. The lions that dominate the two friezes on this jug are recognizably based on creatures which decorated the walls of Assyrian royal palaces in relief sculptures or mosaics of glazed brick. To the lion and the serpent the Corinthian artist has added an imaginary beast, whose two winged and feathered bodies are joined by a single panther's head.

This jug is an example of the so-called black-figure technique, which formed one of the two major styles of Greek vase-painting (the other was known as red-figure). The natural yellowish clay of the Corinth region formed the background, onto which figures were painted in black silhouette. Details were then added by lines incised through the black glaze to the lighter clay beneath, or by areas painted in a contrasting color.

c. 600 B.C. British Museum, London

A CLASH OF WARRIORS

Homer's account in the *Iliad* of part of the last year of the Trojan Was was supplemented by other epics of the seventh and sixth centuries B.C. to form a cycle detailing the entire course of the ten-year struggle. These poems were based on oral tradition dating back perhaps to Mycenaean times, whose events they were believed to reflect. To Homer's audiences, the epics were a historical account of the exploits of their own ancestors in a long-lost heroic age; and the familiarity of episodes from the Trojan War made them favorite subjects for the earliest naturalistic scenes that appeared on Greek pottery.

According to Homer, the Greeks waged their war against Troy to recover Helen, the wife of King Menelaus of Sparta, who had been abducted by Paris, the son of King Priam of Troy. In this painting, on a plate found on the island of Rhodes, Menelaus, on the left, is engaged in hand-to-hand combat with Hector, the foremost Trojan hero. At their feet lies the body of the Trojan warrior Euphorbos, whom Menelaus has slain.

The figures are realistically painted in brownish black with dark red flesh set off against the pale yellow background of the plate. Although the warriors belong to prehistoric times, they bear the armor and weapons of the seventh-century B.C. *hoplite*, or foot soldier. These include a circular shield, a long thrusting spear, a bell-shaped bronze cuirass protecting the upper body, bronze greaves on the legs, and a heavy Corinthian helmet with horsehair crest.

c. 660 B.C. British Museum, London

TEMPLE OF HERA AT OLYMPIA

The Greeks bestowed upon the temples dedicated to their gods an elegance in design and care in craftsmanship that has set them among the foremost splendors of the Classical world. The temple's basic plan consisted of a central sanctuary, or *cella*, and a porch with columns at the front; most temples added a second porch at the back and a colonnade, or peristyle, around all or part of the building. In designing the columns of the temple and the stonework they suport, Greek architects followed closely one of three standard styles, or orders, known as Doric, Ionic, and Corinthian.

The ruined temple of Hera at Olympia in southern Greece shows many of the principal features of the Doric order, the earliest and simplest of the three architectural styles. The Doric column is a sturdy stone pillar rising straight from the platform of the temple, with no separately defined base. Its shaft is fluted and usually consists of several separate drums. A central cavity, visible in the drums of fallen columns that lie in the foreground of the picture, receives a wooden block into which fits a metal dowel, ensuring the precise fit of one drum on top of another. The fluted shaft tapers upward to a top, or capital, consisting of a circular collar, called an *echinus*, and a rectangular block, or *abacus*.

The earliest Greek temples had columns and beams of wood and walls of sun-dried mud brick, and many Greek architectural forms probably derive from the demands of the original wood construction. The abacus, for example, was originally a simple block of wood used to support the architrave. This Temple of Hera originally had wooden columns, replaced at different times by the stone columns which survive today. In front of the temple was a gigantic altar used for sacrifices to Zeus, father of the gods and husband of Hera.

c. 600 B.C.

THE TEMPLES OF HERA
AT PAESTUM IN ITALY

The small city-states in which Greek civilization revived around 800 B.C. sprang up in fertile valleys cut off from one another by high, barren mountains. As their populations grew, lack of space and adequate food supplies forced more and more Greeks to emigrate across the Aegean and the Mediterranean in search of new homes. By the seventh century B.C., colonies throughout the Mediterranean, from Sicily in the west to the Black Sea shores in the east, were trading with the Greek mainland and absorbing its surplus population.

Among the many colonies set up in Italy in the seventh century was that of Poseidonia (known to the Romans as Paestum) in Campania, on the west coast. The temples erected in Paestum over the centuries include two dedicated to Hera, queen of the gods. The two columns in the foreground of this picture belong to the first Temple of Hera, also called the Basilica, which was built in the middle of the sixth century B.C.. Behind are the columns, architrave, and frieze of the second Temple of Hera, which was built in about 430 B.C. and is one of the best preserved of all Doric temples.

The sturdy columns of both temples are nearly seven feet in diameter at the base, and taper upward to the characteristic capital, consisting of echinus and abacus, which supports the architrave, or lowest section, of the entablature. Above the architrave of the second temple runs another typical feature of the Doric order, the frieze, which consists of *metopes*, or open panels, separated from patterns of three vertical grooves, called *triglyphs*. The metopes of many temples were filled with finely carved sculptures.

Visible in the background is the Temple of Ceres, built about 520 B.C.

c. 560-300 B.C.

ARCHAIC SMILE OF A KOUROS

The realistic sculpture of the human figure, which was to be one of the finest achievements of Greek Classical art, originated two centuries earlier in a series of standing male and female stone figures which began to be made in the late seventh century B.C., during the so-called Archaic period of Greek art. These *kouroi* ("youths") and *korai* ("girls") were apparently carved either to represent worshipers in attendance on a god or as commemorative figures to be set on tombs. Some of the male figures may have symbolized Apollo, having been based on earlier wooden effigies of the god.

This marble *kouros* from Boeotia is one of the earliest of these images. The pose, stiff and frontal with left leg advanced, closely resembles that of the carved standing figures of ancient Egypt, with which Greece had close commercial contacts. But whereas the Egyptian standing figures have a supporting pillar and wear at least a kilt, the Greek *kouros* is unsupported and entirely nude. The eyes of this marble youth bulge, and the musculature of his torso is only roughly delineated. The lips are raised at the corners in a characteristic expression that has become known as the Archaic smile. Although the human figure in Egyptian monumental statuary remained stylized throughout the centuries, the Greek sculptors gradually learned how to make their statues anatomically more accurate and their poses more relaxed and naturalistic, thus liberating the figures from the marble and bringing them to vivid life.

c. 560 B.C. British Museum, London

BIRTH OF ATHENA

The black-figure technique of pottery decoration, pioneered in Corinth at the beginning of the seventh century B.C., reached its peak in the potters' workshops of sixth-century Athens. Here, the geometric patterns typical of earlier vases gave way to the represensation of scenes from daily life or from the myths of gods and heroes. The color of the Athenian clay gives a rich red background to the design, against which the detail is painted in a shiny black glaze.

On this Athenian cup, Zeus, the father of the gods, is seen giving birth to Athena. The goddess springs fully grown and armed with a shield from her father's forehead, which Hephaestus (right) has just split open with an ax. Zeus has his divine thunderbolts, but he sits on a chair that could have come from the house of a sixth-century Athenian aristocrat. As in most black-figure pottery, the figures combine head and legs in profile with eye and torso in front view. Red coloring is added to the silhouettes to indicate hair, beards, and tunics; white is used for the female flesh.

Athena, as patron goddess of Athens, is one of the most frequently depicted deities in Attic vase decoration. Her mother was Metis, goddess of wisdom. After Athena was conceived, Zeus swallowed Metis whole in case she bore him a son; for a prophesy had foretold that such a son would replace Zeus as supreme ruler of the world. Athena inherited her mother's role as goddess of wisdom and intellect. She was also seen as the patron goddess of useful crafts such as agriculture and weaving, and among many inventions attributed to her was the potter's wheel.

c. 560-550 B.C. British Museum, London

THESEUS AND THE MINOTAUR

The fine glaze on this black-figure wine jar, undimmed after 2,500 years, is a tribute to the skills of the sixth-century B.C. Athenian potter and the artist who worked with him. The coloring was achieved through the use of a "slip," or light coating of diluted clay, and the skillful adjustment of the heat in the pottery kiln during firing. Even with the technical developments of the present day, modern experts have been unable to reproduce the glaze precisely.

The scene on the vase is Theseus' slaying of the Minotaur, a part-bull part-human monster on the island of Crete. Theseus, a legendary king of Athens, volunteered in his youth to be one of a band of fourteen young prisoners whom the Athenians had to send to Crete as a sacifice to the Minotaur. Theseus penetrated the labyrinth in which the monster was kept, killed it with his sword, and then escaped through the labyrinth with the aid of a thread given to him by Ariadne, daughter of the Cretan king Minos.

To create his painting, the artist first coated the unornamented parts of the vase and the silhouettes of his design with diluted clay; then the potter fired the pot in his kiln to a temperature of 800 degrees Centigrade. The iron in the clay absorbed oxygen from the air, turning the painted areas deep red and the remainder of the vase a reddish brown. Next the potter closed the vents of the kiln and raised the internal temperature even higher; this forced the oxygen out, turning the pot black. When the vents were opened and oxygen was readmitted, the unpainted areas of the vase turned reddish-brown again, but the painted areas had acquired a laminated surface, not allowing oxygen to pass through, and so remained black.

550 B.C. British Museum, London

WARRIOR OF THE HEROIC AGE

The artists who decorated Greek pottery excelled at fitting their designs into the precise area available on a particular cup or vase. Some of the finest examples of this skill are the scenes created for the circular field inside the *kylix*, a shallow drinking cup which came into use in Athens in the sixth century B.C. The warrior on the attack in this cup is captured in a whirl of arms, spear, and legs that must have seemed to leap into life as the drinker saw it through his wine.

The warrior is marked as a figure of Greece's earlier heroic age by his oval Boeotian shield, quite unlike the circular shield borne by the hoplite, or foot soldier, of later Greek fighting forces. This oval shield may have been the artist's way of suggesting the giant figure-of-eight shield, almost the height of a man, behind which the warriors of Mycenaean times sheltered themselves. The warrior in the painting has one arm thrust through a strap on the inside of the shield, and his fingers grip a loop on its rim. His other arm is drawn back, ready to administer an underarm thrust with his long, metal-tipped wooden spear. The panther skin he wears emphasizes his heroic status. His helmet, however, was typical of sixth-century Corinth, made of bronze and topped by a horsehair crest.

c. 550 B.C. British Museum, London

38

ACHILLES SLAYING PENTHESILEIA

One of the finest of all Athenian vase painters working in the black-figure technique was Exekias, who here shows the hero Achilles slaying Penthesileia, queen of the Amazons. The figures on this wine jar, found at Vulci in Etruria, are dramatically arranged against the red background, and delicate patterns incised through the black glaze render the decoration of Penthesileia's costume in rich detail. Red paint gives a three-dimensional solidity to the shields, while the flesh of Penthesileia is painted white, a convention in the portrayal of women on black-figure vases. The two figures are identified by their names inscribed beside them; the potter and artist has also signed his own name, *Exekias epoiesen*, "Exekias made it," to the left of Achilles.

The Amazons were a legendary race of female warriors of Cappadocia, in Asia Minor. According to tradition, female children had their right breasts cut off to enable them to use use bow and arrows more easily: the Greek word *amazon* means "breastless." The Amazons were perpetually at enmity with the Greeks, and in the Trojan War Penthesileia led them to the assistance of Troy after Achilles had killed the Trojan hero Hector. Greek tradition depicts Achilles as falling in love with Penthesileia at the moment of slaying her, as he recognizes the Amazon queen's beauty and courage. To contemporaries familiar with the story, the gleaming eye with which Exekias shows Achilles fixing Penthesileia would have powerfully evoked the turmoil of fierceness, love, and remorse in the hero's mind.

c. 540 B.C. British Museum, London

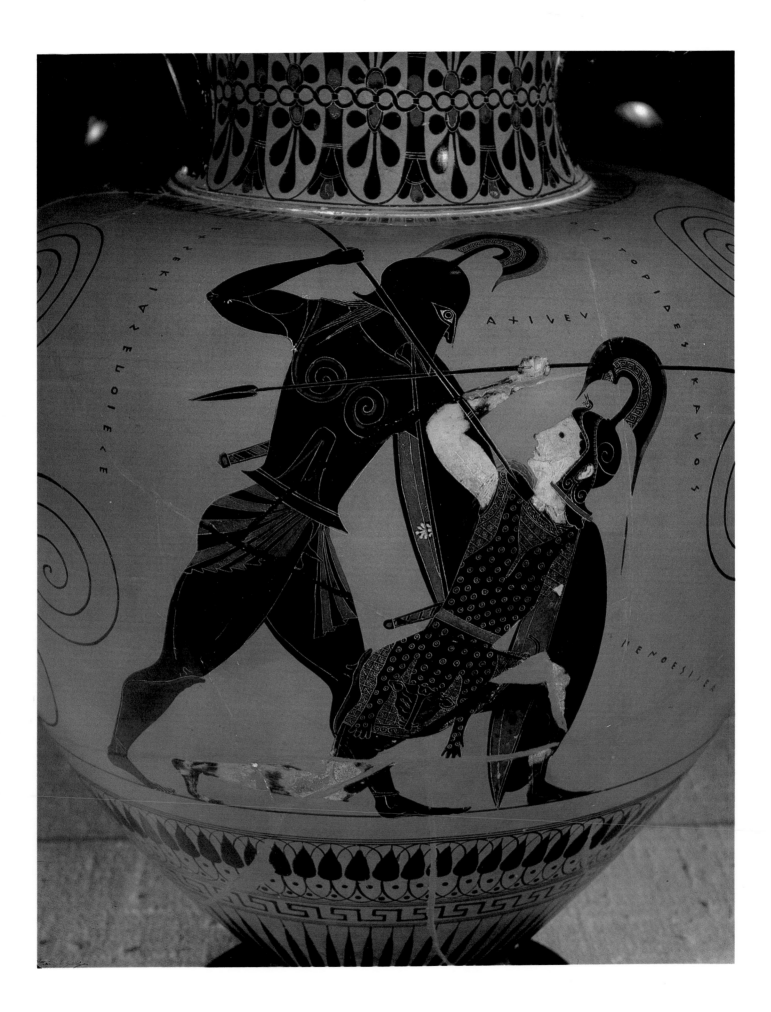

MERCHANT BOAT

The ancient Greeks early became masters of the sea. Colonists sailed out from overcrowded city-states to found settlements abroad, and in their wake merchants traded Greek wine, olive oil, and pottery for grain, timber, metals, and other raw materials from all around the shores of the Mediterranean. Even for Greeks in their homeland, it was easier to transport goods by sea, hugging the coast, than to try to carry them across the high mountain passes that separated one city-state from another.

Various types of boats were developed for the different purposes of fishing, trade, and battle. The vessel at sea painted on this black-figure cup is a deep-bellied merchant ship. Unlike the lighter galleys built for speed in battle and powered by oarsmen, the heavy oak-built merchant vessel had no oars and depended for propulsion on its single square linen sail. When the wind was unfavorable, the ship's crew could only reef the sail with hempen ropes and wait for it to change. The horizontal lines running the length of the vessel in this painting appear to be the rails of a catwalk above the unfloored cargo space; the crisscross lines below it represent the freight lashed into place. A ladder for embarking and disembarking hangs at the stern over the head of the steersman, who controls the steering oars on either side of the stern.

To protect their merchant fleets from pirates and defend their shores against invaders, the Greeks used fast, light galleys propelled by oars. The early bireme had 50 oars; the larger trireme was about 120 feet long and powered by 170 oarsmen. Both types of warship had a bronze spike on the prow to ram enemy vessels. Crewed by skilled Athenian seamen, the powerful triremes won the decisive sea battle against the Persians at Salamis in 480 B.C.

c. 540 B.C. British Museum, London

42

BIRTHPLACE OF THE OLYMPIC GAMES

Through this vaulted passageway athletes entered the stadium at Olympia from the *altis*, or sacred grove, to test their physique and skill against competitors from all over the Greek world in the quadrennial Olympic Games. For five days, competitors battled in a variety of athletic contests and chariot races before an audience of more than 50,000 watching from the slopes around the stadium.

The Greeks set a high value on physical prowess, and from earliest times athletic contests formed part of religious festivals held throughout Greece. Special importance was attached to the four regular festivals at Olympia, Delphi, Nemea, and the Isthmus of Corinth. For these so-called Panhellenic Games, a truce was declared in wars between rival city-states so that contestants could travel in safety to and from the Games.

The Olympic Games, inaugurated in 776 B.C., were dedicated to Zeus, and opening and closing religious ceremonies were held at the nearby sanctuary of the father of the gods. The winner of each competitive event received a crown of wild olive leaves, but his real reward was the glory of having striven in honor of the gods and having demonstrated his superiority over his rivals. The Games were held every four years until A.D. 393, when the Roman emperor Theodosius ended them; the modern Olympics date from 1896.

Fourth century B.C.

RUNNERS IN THE PANATHENAIC GAMES

Aside from the great Games at Olympia, which attracted contestants from all over the Greek world, all other cities held festivals that included athletic contests. One of these was the Great Panathenaea, held in Athens every fourth year in honor of the city's patron goddess, Athena. This painting shows three runners battling for supremacy in a foot race at the Panathenaic games. The decoration appears on one of the prize amphorae which, filled with olive oil, were presented to winners in the games—the olive tree being the gift with which, according to myth, Athena endowed her city.

The lines incised into the black silhouettes are accurate in anatomical detail, and contrive to suggest economically yet vividly the strenuousness of the contestants' struggle. The foot race was a feature of Greek athletic contests from the time the Olympic Games began in 776 B.C. For the first fourteen Olympiads, the only event was the *stadion*, a 200-yard sprint down one length of a sanded course; a *stade*, the Greeks' principal measure of distance, was just over 600 feet. Later variations included a two-*stade* race, down the course and back; a four-*stade* event; and an endurance test over twenty-four *stades*, or 5,000 yards. Starting and finishing lines were usually marked by stone slabs across the track, with parallel grooves cut into the stone to act as starting blocks. Athletes always competed naked in the Games, and the artist here expresses the admiration Greeks felt for the human body at the peak of physical perfection.

336 B.C. British Museum, London

DELPHI CHARIOTEER

The confident gaze of a triumphant charioteer, his head wreathed by a victor's woolen fillet, is captured in this fine bronze statue found at Delphi. Most of the major series of athletic games in ancient Greece opened with a chariot race; competing chariots from all over the Greek world, drawn by teams of two or four horses, careered up and down a fixed course in a nine-mile race which few completed. The inscription on the base of this lifesize statue states that it was made to commemorate a victory in the Delphi games by Polyzalus, the ruler of Gela in Sicily. The charioteer stands upright to hold the reins of his team of four horses, as if parading in a lap of honor after his triumph. The statue was intended to be set in the sanctuary of Apollo as an offering to the god, in whose honor the games were held.

The bronze charioteer is an example of the early Classical style; the sculptor has relaxed the stiff frontal pose of Archaic statuary to present his subject in a more lifelike stance, his head slightly turned to the right. It embodies an idealized form of beauty beloved by Greek sculptors of the period, and the serenity of the features is emphasized by the even folds of the charioteer's long *chiton*, with its high belt. The intensity of his gaze is enhanced by the white enamel eyes set in brown stone. The copper eyelashes and the side locks of hair were made separately from the head and attached after casting.

c. 474 B.C. Delphi Museum

MULETEER AT THE GAMES

The oil-filled amphorae presented to winners of the Games at the Great Panathenaea in Athens had a painting of the goddess Athena on one side, and on the other a representation of the event for which the prize was awarded. This amphora, painstakingly reassembled from fragments, shows a driver crouched in a light racing cart drawn by two prancing mules.

Chariot races featured in Greek games from earliest days; Homer, in his *Iliad*, describes them as taking place before the walls of Troy as the Greeks mourned their dead hero Patroclus. Races with four-horse chariots were part of the Olympic Games as early as 680 B.C., but the *apene*, or race with paired mules, was not introduced until the sixth century. The muleteer rode seated, unlike the standing charioteer of the horse-drawn chariot, and often dangled a carrot in front of his team to spur the animals onward. The winning driver received a woolen headband; the olive-leaf crown of victory went to the owner of the winning team.

In addition to racing, chariots were also used for ceremonial purposes. In parades such as that of the Great Panathenaea in Athens, armed warriors stood beside the charioteer and leaped on and off the moving chariots.

c. 550 B.C. British Museum, London

JAVELIN THROWING ON HORSEBACK

The ancient Greeks made great use of horses. Despite the mountainous terrain, much traveling within Greece was done on horseback, and goods for trade were conveyed between city-states by light carts drawn by horses or mules. Horse races and chariot races figured prominently in organized games, and equestrian skill was respected as highly as accomplishment in other forms of athletics. Jockeys competed without saddle or stirrups, riding up to twelve laps on an 800-yard course.

One variation on the horse race, introduced to the Panathenaic Games in Athens in the fifth century B.C., was the mounted javelin-throwing contest, depicted on this prize oil amphora. The Greeks used two types of javelin in fighting and hunting: the heavy *enchos* for hand-to-hand fighting, and the lighter *akon*, a throwing weapon. The *akon* used in athletic contests was a wooden javelin up to six feet long, with a noose halfway along the shaft to enable the thrower to give it added momentum. The mounted *akontists* in the painting are clad in the *chlamys*, or long riding cloak, and *petasos*, or peaked cap, of the traveler. A shield fixed to a post serves as a target.

Late fifth century B.C. British Museum, London

BOXERS AT THE GAMES

From the use of his own fist as man's earliest weapon, boxing developed as one of the most ancient sports. Boxing matches were a feature of Greek athletic contests from earliest times. Homer, in the *Iliad*, describes a boxing match that took place during funeral games in honor of the dead Patroclus, before the gates of besieged Troy. On that occasion both winner and loser were rewarded, the winner with a mule, the loser with a drinking cup. The boxers exchanging blows on this Athenian vase wear *himantes*, gloves formed of oxhide bindings laced around their hands. Greek boxers were not confined to a ring or limited to timed rounds; the contestants simply fought on, ranging back and forth across the stadium, until one was vanquished. However, the most dangerous punches were banned, and a boxer who killed his opponent was deemed the loser for breaking the rules.

This small black-figure amphora bears the prominent legend *Nikosthenes epoiesen*, "Nikosthenes made it." Nikosthenes was one of the most prolific of sixth-century Athenian potters; more than a hundred of his vases survive, decorated by a variety of painters. As in most black-figure painting, head and legs appear in profile, and chest, shoulders, and eyes are in front view. Incised lines are used for the boxers' hand bindings, and red paint for their hair and beards—and for the bleeding nose of the losing contestant.

c. 525 B.C. British Museum, London

PANKRATIASTS AT THE ATHENS GAMES

One of the toughest of the Greeks' organized games was the *pankration*, a form of man-to-man unarmed combat in which almost any form of aggression was allowed. Contestants wrestled, boxed, kicked, hit, and tried to strangle each other; the only prohibited forms of assault were biting an opponent and gouging his eyes out. Even when the combatants fell to the ground, the struggle went on until one contestant conceded defeat by raising his index finger. The *pankration* was supervised by an umpire holding a rod.

Even the more orthodox form of wrestling that formed part of the five-event Pentathlon was a rough contest by modern standards. No holds were barred, tripping an opponent was allowed, and three falls gained the victory.

This black-figure painting of the *pankration* appears on an amphora, or oil jar, given to the victor in that event at the quadrennial Great Panathenaea in Athens. The black-figure technique of pottery decoration was retained for these prize amphorae at the Panathenaic Games until well into the second century B.C., long after the red-figure had superseded it for other types of vases.

c. 330 B.C. British Museum, London

ATHLETES OF THE PENTHATHLON

All around excellence in athletics was tested by the Pentathlon—a contest requiring competitors to excel in a series of five different events. Introduced into contests as early as 700 B.C., the Pentathlon comprised the long jump, a foot race of up to 400 yards, discus throwing, javelin throwing, and wrestling.

In this painting on an Athenian prize amphora, the long-jumper on the left holds two *halteres*—weights of lead or stone which were swung forward to give added impetus to the jump. The javelin held by the second and fourth figures was about a man's height, made of wood and tipped with metal; it was thrown by two fingers inserted into a thong wound around the center of the missile. The discus, held by the third figure, was a circular stone or bronze plate weighing about nine pounds, probably thrown underarm.

To win the Pentathlon, an athlete had to take first place in three of the five events. The order in which the events were contested is uncertain, but it is believed they may have started with the long jump, discus, and javelin. If one contestant won all three field events he became the outright winner of the Pentathlon. If, however, different athletes won the three events, then victory was decided by a runoff contest consisting of a foot race and a wrestling match.

520 B.C. British Museum, London

FEMALE ATHLETE

Only males competed in the formal athletic games of ancient Greece, but in the sternly disciplined city-state of Sparta, girls as well underwent hard physical training to ensure that they should bear fit and strong children. The young girl represented in this bronze statuette, only four and a half inches high, is believed to be a Spartan. She is one of several running female figures attached to the rim of the lid of a large bronze vase found at Prisren in Yugoslavia. The girl runner wears a short *chiton*, which leaves her right shoulder and breast bare, and she lifts the hem of the chiton to make running easier. The blend of front-view shoulders with left-profile head and right-profile legs produces an awkward stance that falls short of the naturalism achieved later in the finest works of the Classical period.

The city-state of Sparta, in the Laconian area of the Peloponnese, was renowned for the courage and skill of its fighting men. All boys were taken from their mothers at the age of seven and trained in military camps whose harsh discipline has made "Spartan" a byword for stern austerity and contempt for physical comforts. The military nature of Spartan society probably developed from the need of the state to control a huge subject population of serfs, who greatly outnumbered their rulers. Their military skills gave the Spartans a leading role in the Greeks' victory over the invading Persians in 480-479 B.C., and then enabled them to defeat their Athenian rivals, in the ensuing Peloponnesian War.

c. 520 B.C. British Museum, London

SCYTHIAN ARCHER

A bowman draws an arrow from his quiver on the run in this spirited painting signed by Epiktetos, one of the earliest masters of the red-figure style of pottery decoration. The figure is at once realistic and graceful; the painter has captured the archer in a lively attitude and has rendered the details of his oriental costume with a delicate touch. The bow is painted in purple for added contrast, and the entire composition is skillfully fitted into the circular framework of a plate.

Archers and lead-shot slingers were extensively used by the armies of the Greek city-states to support their troops of heavily armed foot soldiers. Most of the bowmen were recruited from the Scythians, a race of nomads who ranged widely across the northern Balkans and the shores of the Black Sea and were skilled horsemen and archers. They used the curiously curved bow, with its forward-pointing horns, that became familar as the "Cupid's bow" of Greek painting. It had a wooden core strengthened by strips of horn and animal sinew, and the bowman had to use both legs and arms to compress the bow enough to string it. It could shoot an arrow nearly 200 yards.

The bowman's long patterned trousers and high-crowned cap are typically Scythian; so too is the "bearded" quiver and bow container, worn at waist level instead of on the back in the manner of Greek archers.

c. 520 B.C. British Museum, London

HERACLES AND THE NEMEAN LION

Heracles was one of the most widely revered of all Greek heroes for his courage and strength, and his mythical Twelve Labors are the subjects of innumerable Athenian black-figure vase paintings. The son of Zeus by Alcmene, Heracles was commanded by the ruler Eurystheus to undertake twelve mighty tasks as the price of his freedom. The first of these labors, illustrated on this vase, was to kill a monstrous lion that lived in the valley of Nemea in the Peloponnese. Heracles attacked the beast first with a club cut from the Nemean woods and then with a bow and arrows; but the lion proved invulnerable to weapons, and so Heracles finally wrestled with it and strangled it with his bare hands. Watching the struggle are Heracles' comrade Iolaos and the armed figure of Athena, Heracles' divine ally and protectress. Heracles skinned the vanquished lion and wore the skin as a protection during his subsequent labors.

The figures are shown in profile, except for the frontal eyes. Supplementing the incised detail of the bodies, red paint is used for the male figures' beards (a conventional symbol of age). Athena's flesh is rendered in white.

c. 510 B.C. British Museum, London

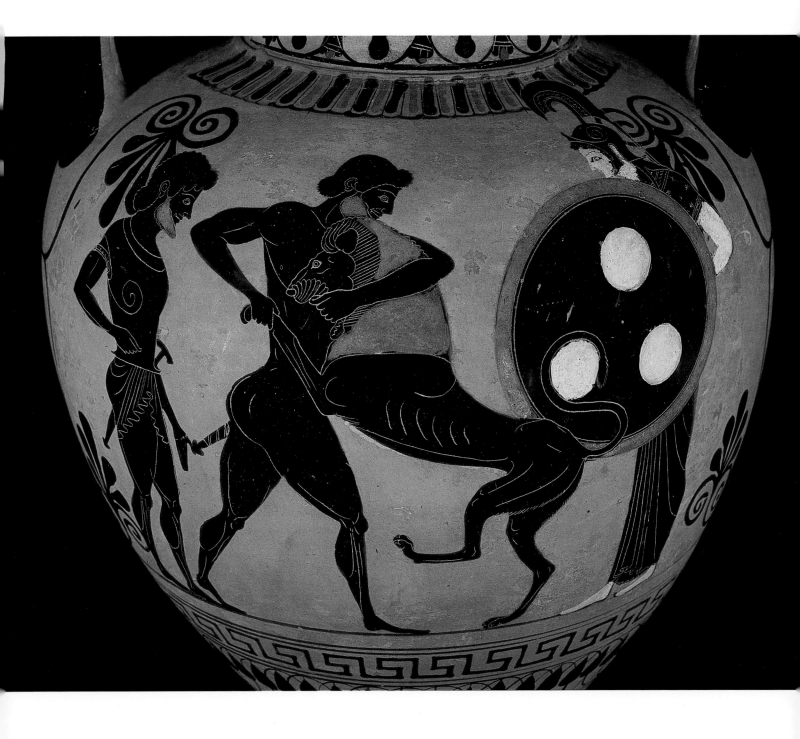

HERACLES AND THE CRETAN BULL

After killing the Nemean lion, Heracles set forth on the remainder of his Twelve Labors at the command of King Eurystheus. He vanquished the many-headed Hydra of the Lernaean swamp; he captured the Arcadian stag, after pursuing it for a year; he trapped a wild boar among the snows of Mount Erymanthus; he cleansed the stables of King Augeus of the accumulated filth of thirty years by diverting two rivers to run through them; and he killed the man-eating birds of Lake Stymphalus.

The seventh labor of Heracles, the capture of the Cretan bull, is the subject of this black-figure painting on an Athenian *olpe*, or wine jug. The bull was the gift of Poseidon, god of the sea, to King Minos of Crete as a sacrifice to the gods. Captivated by the animal's beauty, Minos kept the bull and sacrificed another in its place. In revenge, Poseidon drove the bull mad. Heracles captured it and brought it to Greece, where he set it free.

Five more labors awaited Heracles before he earned the freedom Eurystheus had promised. He tamed the man-eating mares of the Thracian king Diomedes and fed their master to them; seized the girdle of Hippolyta, queen of the Amazons; took the oxen belonging to the three-bodied monster Geryon; persuaded Atlas to fetch the golden apples of the Hesperides, while he held up the heavens in Atlas' place; and descended into the lower world to capture Cerberus, the three-headed hound that guarded the entrance into Hades.

500-490 B.C. British Museum, London

66

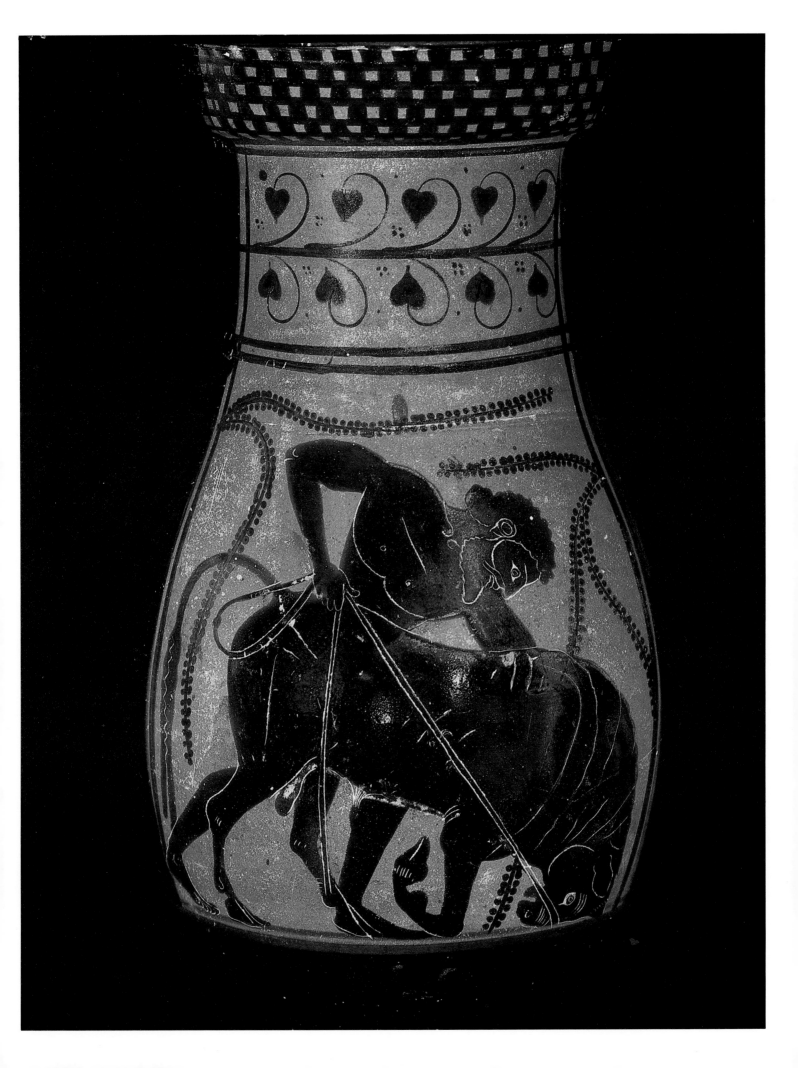

TEMPLE OF ATHENA-APHAIA

The bold, simple lines of the Doric order of architecture are well represented in this temple on the island of Aegina. Six fluted columns of local limestone at each end and twelve along each side (instead of the more usual thirteen) formed a covered colonnade around the central *cella*, or shrine. The temple is dedicated to Aphaia, thought to be a local deity associated with the widely worshipped goddess Athena.

The triangular pediments over the eastern and western entrances of the temple were decorated with marble statues representing battles between Greeks and Trojans before the walls of besieged Troy, with the figure of Athena, protectress of the Greeks in the Trojan War, at the center. Surviving parts of these statues are now in Munich.

The temple stands on high ground in the northeast corner of Aegina, which lies in the Saronic Gulf just south of Athens and Piraeus, its seaport. From the seventh century B.C., Aegina was a prosperous city-state and an artistic and commercial center of importance. Its growing wealth, based on trade with Greek colonies overseas, brought it into frequent clashes with nearby Athens. Pericles called Aegina "the eyesore of the Piraeus," and in 456 B.C. he absorbed it into the growing Athenian empire.

c. 510 B.C.

HEAD OF THE GORGON

A familiar motif of Greek vase painting and sculpture was the *gorgoneion*—a demonic head with boarlike tusks, protruding tongue, and hair of entwined serpents. It took its name from the myth of the Gorgons, three ferocious sisters whose look had the power to turn men into stone. (One of the Gorgons, Medusa, was beheaded by the hero Perseus.)

This *gorgoneion*, on an Attic water jar found at Tarquinia in Italy, is a striking example of red-figure painting—the second of the two major styles of pottery decoration in ancient Greece. The new technique was first developed in Athens around 530 B.C., and gradually superseded black-figure work as the most popular style of vase painting. Red-figure vases are so called because on them the figures appear in the natural red color of the clay, while the background is painted black. Lines of detail are painted in with glaze, giving the artist much greater opportunity for subtle, realistic effects than the incising tool used in black-figure painting.

The painting is by one of the finest and most prolific of red-figure artists; more than 250 surviving vases have been attributed to him. He worked in the first quarter of the fifth century B.C. and is known as the Berlin Painter, after a tall amphora of his that stands in the Berlin Museum.

c. 490 B.C. British Museum, London

PERSEUS WITH THE HEAD OF MEDUSA

One of the most popular heroes of Greek mythology was Perseus, the son of Zeus and Danae. This red-figure painting on a water jar made in southern Italy depicts the most famous of the exploits of Perseus: his seizing of the head of the Gorgon Medusa.

The Gorgons were three monstrous sisters with wings, claws, scaly bodies, and hair of entwined snakes. Of the three sisters—Medusa, Stheno, and Euryale—only Medusa was a mortal woman. The goddess Athena turned Medusa into a monster after she had profaned one of Athena's temples by mating there with Poseidon, god of the sea. Perseus was sent by Polydectes, king of the island of Seriphos where Perseus was brought up, to slay Medusa and bring back her head. The face of a Gorgon turned to stone anyone who looked directly at it; but Perseus used a polished bronze shield, the gift of Athena, as a mirror in which he could watch Medusa's reflection unscathed as he cut off her head. According to the myth, two offspring, the monster Chrysaor and Pegasus, the winged horse, leaped from Medusa's body as her head was struck off.

Perseus also had winged sandals and a helmet that made him invisible to help him escape the pursuit of the other two Gorgons. Even in death, Medusa's head retained its lethal power, and Perseus used the head as a weapon in his subsequent adventures before giving it to Athena to place in the middle of her breastplate.

350-330 B.C. British Museum, London

A DIVINE GIFT TO MANKIND

Man's earliest civilized settlements sprang up around organized farming communities. The Greeks recognized man's debt to agriculture by the special reverence they accorded to Demeter, the goddess of agriculture, and her daughter Persephone. This painting shows the way in which, according to Greek myth, the goddesses passed the secret of agriculture to mankind.

The seated figure is Triptolemus, the mythical king of Eleusis, a coastal city northwest of Athens. He is flanked by Demeter (left) and Persephone, holding burning torches. Demeter has given Triptolemus ears of wheat and a winged chariot, in which he is to ride across the earth to bring men the secrets of agriculture. He holds a shallow bowl into which Persephone pours a libation to endow his mission with success.

The worship of Demeter and Persephone at Eleusis, said to have been established by Triptolemus himself, became one of the most important cults in Greece. Festivals in honor of the goddesses were attended by rites so secret in character that they were referred to as the Eleusinian Mysteries, and the penalty for initiates who betrayed the secrets to outsiders was death.

This painting, on a large *skyphos*, or drinking cup, is by Makron, perhaps the most prolific of red-figure painters. His vases were valued so highly for the skill with which he painted the folds and decorations of drapery that they were placed in tombs to equip the dead for the afterlife; this example was found in a tomb at Capua in Italy.

490-480 B.C. British Museum, London

ODYSSEUS AND THE TROJAN SPY

Athenian artists were the most prolific exponents of red-figure vase decoration, and the products of their workshops were exported widely throughout the Mediterranean world for two centuries. The only other part of the Greek world that produced good-quality red-figure vases was southern Italy, where the spread of the technique may have been connected with the arrival of migrant potters and painters from Athens around 440 B.C.

This painting on a vase from Lucenia shows an incident which, according to Homer's *Iliad*, took place toward the end of the long Trojan War, when the Greeks were encamped on the plain before the walls of besieged Troy. The Greek hero Odysseus (left) and his companion Diomedes (right) are shown on an armed reconnaissance into the Trojan lines, where they ambush Dolon, a spy on a similar mission for the Trojans. According to Homer, the two Greeks cut Dolon's throat after torturing him to reveal the where-abouts of King Rhesus of Thrace, ally of the Trojans. Hiding Dolon's bow and spear and his skin cloak and cap in a bush, Odysseus and Diomedes then hurried on to King Rhesus's camp, where they killed the king and his companions and stole their horses. On the way back to their own camp, the Greeks recovered the possessions of the murdered Dolon.

The theatrical postures of the characters in the painting suggest that the artist may have been portraying a scene from a play, attributed to Euripides, that was based on the same events as those narrated in the *Iliad*. The coloring is typical of Italian vases: the black glaze is less shiny than that of Athenian wares, and the figures reflect the lighter color of Italian clay.

400-370 B.C. British Museum, London

ODYSSEUS AND THE SIRENS

The time span of the *Iliad* covers only fifty days during the last year of the Trojan War; yet by skillful use of flashbacks, Homer manages to sketch the broad canvas of the entire ten-year struggle. The wanderings of the Greek warrior Odysseus on his way back to his island home of Ithaca after the war were to occupy another ten years; and again, in his *Odyssey*, Homer has compressed the adventures which occurred on the long voyage into an epic whose action is concentrated into only forty days.

The design on this vase depicts an adventure from the twelfth book of the *Odyssey*. Odysseus and his companions are carried by the wind to the island of the Sirens, winged creatures with the heads of beautiful women, whose sweet songs lure men to destruction on the rocky shore. Odysseus, renowned for his cunning, has stopped the ears of his companions with wax and has himself tied to the pinewood mast of his boat. Deaf to the songs of the Sirens, the oarsmen row on unharmed; the rear oarsman looks over his shoulder to exhort his colleagues. Because Odysseus himself has heard the Sirens' songs and survived, one Siren hurls herself to her death.

The painting is on a *stamnos*, a two-handled vase for storing wine or oil, squatter than the more common amphora. Artists of red-figure vases have sometimes been named after their best-known work; hence the artist of this vase is called the Siren Painter. Framing the central panel showing the human adventurers is a border based on the meander pattern, retained from vases of the Geometric period.

490-480 B.C. British Museum, London

MEDEA AND THE RAM

In his celebrated quest for the Golden Fleece, the hero Jason was helped by the magic arts of the sorceress Medea, the daughter of Aeetes, king of Colchis. In this vase painting, Medea demonstrates how she can restore lost youth to a living body. She has cut up a ram and placed it in a cauldron of boiling water; the ram emerges from the cauldron not only whole but rejuvenated, through the addition of a magic potion which Medea is adding from the container in her hand.

The painter has left it unclear who is the subject of this particular rejuvenation spell. The figure on the right is named "Jason"; this may have been a mistake for Aeson, the father of Jason, for whose benefit Medea is said to have worked her spell after returning to Greece as Jason's wife. However, another legend says that on his return to Greece Jason found his father murdered by the tyrant and usurper Pelias. According to this account, Medea demonstrated her spell to the daughters of Pelias and then told them that they could rejuvenate their own father by cutting him in pieces and boiling him like the ram. The daughter, persuaded, slew their father and placed his dismembered body in a cauldron—but Medea than refused to add the magic potion.

c. 470 B.C. British Museum, London

THE CHATSWORTH APOLLO

Greek sculptors used bronze for their statues as commonly as they used marble. Few of the great bronze-cast statues have survived, however, for bronze was highly prized in medieval times for the making of weapons, and countless works of art were melted down for their metal.

A fine example of the high standard of craftsmanship achieved in bronze is provided by this head found at Tamassos (present-day Politiko) in Cyprus. It is part of a statue representing the god Apollo and set in one of the god's many sanctuaries. In its serene dignity it embodies the idealized form of beauty typical of the early Classical period. The profile is typically Grecian, the forehead and nose forming an almost unbroken straight line. The head, slightly larger than lifesize, is often called the "Chatsworth Head," because it was kept for many years at Chatsworth House in Derbyshire, England. Eyes, probably of glass and painted marble, once gleamed from the now-empty sockets, and lashes were set into small bronze plates round the eyes. The ornate locks of hair were separately cast and then attached to the head.

The head was made, like most Greek bronzes, by the "lost wax" method. The figure was first modeled in wax, then coated with clay to form a mold. The wax was then removed from the mold, either by heating the figure and letting the wax run out through holes in the casing, or else by separating the mold into pieces and removing the original carved figure from within. The mold was then lined with wax to the required thickness of the bronze of the finished statue and a new clay core was inserted, kept at a fixed distance from the mold by bronze bars. The mold and its core were then heated to let the wax run out, and molten bronze was poured into the mold to replace the lost wax. When the metal had hardened, the casing was broken away and the pieces of the core picked out in lumps.

c. 470-460 B.C. British Museum, London

APHRODITE RIDING ON A GOOSE

As a variation on black-figure and red-figure pottery decoration, a technique known as "white ground" was developed by Athenian potters during the late sixth century B.C. A "slip" of diluted white clay was applied to a vase to create a background for the design, which was then added in lines of colored glaze.

The figure on the inside of this *kylix*, or drinking cup, is Aphrodite, goddess of love and beauty, who is riding majestically through the skies on the back of a goose. The scene symbolizes Aphrodite's supposed power over all the creatures of the animal world. The decoration is attributed to an artist called the Pistoxenos Painter, one of the most skillful exponents of the white-ground technique. The delicacy of the painting gives some hint of the artistic skill that artists of the time must also have brought to larger-scale paintings, which have not survived.

There were numerous cults of Aphrodite in ancient Greece, some of them based on fertility cults originating in the Near East. Some myths portrayed Aphrodite as the daughter of Zeus; others said she was born from the foam of sea—hence her name, derived from the Greek *aphros*, "foam." With Athena and Hera, Aphrodite was one of the three rival goddesses whose claim to supreme beauty was put to the judgment of Paris. Swayed by Aphrodite's promise to help him to win the fairest of mortal women for his wife, Paris judged in her favor. The goddess then helped Paris to carry off Helen, wife of the Spartan king Menelaus; this abduction was the legendary cause of the Trojan War.

c. 470-460 B.C. British Museum, London

CORINTHIAN BRONZE HELMET

This heavy warrior's helmet, hammered out of a single sheet of bronze, is a fine example of the highly functional art of the Greek metalsmith. This type of helmet, believed to have been developed in Corinth, was widely adopted as the standard helmet of the Greek *hoplite*, or heavily armed foot soldier.

In battle the Corinthian helmet, with its long nose-piece and projecting cheek guards, covered most of the face, leaving only the eyes clear. It was lined with leather and topped by a crest of horsehair. The helmet's drawback was that the wearer could not hear through it, so whenever he was not in action the *hoplite* pushed it back onto the top of his head.

This particular helmet was found at Olympia, and an inscription records that it was dedicated to Zeus by the people of Argos, as spoil taken in war by the Argives during one of their frequent battles with the forces of rival Corinth. The city-states of ancient Greece were often at war with one another, and the armies of the main city-states, such as Athens and Sparta, formed disciplined fighting forces that stood the Greeks in good stead against the Persian invaders of the fifth century B.C.

Early fifth century B.C. British Museum, London

POSEIDON, GOD OF THE SEA

This majestic head, its human features bearing the added stamp of divinity, is believed to represent Poseidon, brother of Zeus and god of the sea. Appropriately, it was from the depths of the Aegean Sea off the north coast of Euboea that the bronze statue was recovered in modern times. The statue, which stands nearly seven feet tall, was probably part of a shipment of sculptures produced by the craftsmen of Attica for markets overseas; or, it may have been a consignment of booty seized by the conquering Romans.

The regal stare and powerful muscles of the god provide striking evidence of the developing skills of Greek sculptors during the early Classical period, and make this one of the finest of all Greek statues in bronze. Gone is the fixed, frontal pose and the unnatural smile of Archaic times; this face achieves a vivid realism, and the eyeballs of colored stone which originally filled the sockets, rimmed by brows inlaid with other metals, must have struck awe into the heart of the beholder.

The god's head is turned sharply left to look along his left arm at an adversary, and his right arm is poised to hurl a deadly trident at his target. The weapon itself is lost; some scholars have speculated that it may have been not a trident but a thunderbolt, so that the figure would be Zeus, king of the gods, rather than his brother Poseidon.

c. 460 B.C. National Museum, Athens

BATTLE OF THE
CENTAURS AND THE LAPITHS

Around the outside of the Parthenon—the mighty temple to Athena built on the Acropolis in Athens—runs a Doric frieze consisting of ninety-two separate sculptured metopes, or marble panels, depicting episodes from Greek mythology. This panel, from a series on the south side of the temple, shows a scene in the mythical struggle between the Centaurs and the Lapiths: a Centaur leaps triumphantly upon a falling Lapith, who gropes for a rock to fend off his attacker.

According to tradition, an early ruler of the Lapiths mated with a cloud to produce the savage Centaurs, part horse and part human, who lived on Mount Pelion and challenged the Lapiths for a share in their kingdom. When Pirithous, king of the Lapiths, invited the Centaurs to his marriage feast, the Centaurs got drunk and attempted to carry off the Lapith women. The ensuing fight, a favorite subject of Greek artists and sculptors, ended in the defeat of the Centaurs and their exile from their country.

The panel is four feet square and sculpted in high relief; the heads are carved in the round, like those of freestanding sculptures, and the figures are joined to the marble background only below the shoulders. The Centaur is depicted with as much attention to detail as the Lapith, for to the sculptor the human and part-human characters of Greek myth were equally real.

In choosing the subjects for the outer frieze of the Parthenon, Pericles and his principal sculptor, Phidias, were intent on glorifying Greece's recent triumph over the Persian invaders by likening it to the earlier triumphs of mythical Greek heroes over barbarian forces. Accordingly, other sections of the frieze show the victory of the gods of Mount Olympus over the Giants; the capture of Troy (which gave the Greeks of Mycenaean times victory in the Trojan War); and the successful defense of Athens by Theseus and his men against the invading Amazons.

c. 445 B.C. British Museum, London

TERPSICHORE,
MUSE OF DANCE AND SONG

The scene on this red-figure vase painting expresses the reverence that ancient Greeks felt for music, as an art form inspired by the gods. Terpsichore, the Muse of dance and song, is seated playing the harp. Listening are her attendants Melousa (left), holding an *aulos* or double flute, and Musaios, holding a lyre. Above Terpsichore's head is another stringed instrument, a cradle cithara.

The lyre was one of the most widely used of all Greek musical instruments, and its use as an accompaniment to the chanting of poetry of thought and emotion gave the name of lyric poetry to this type of literature. According to Greek legend, the lyre was invented by Hermes, messenger of the gods, as a childhood toy. He hollowed out a tortoise and covered its shell in oxhide to make a soundbox, then attached a framework of wooden horns to the shell and stretched chords of cow gut across it. The tortoise shell soundbox is clearly visible in this painting. The cithara at the top of the picture is similar to the lyre but made with a wooden soundbox that more strongly amplified the notes and was therefore particularly suited to accompany recital of epic poetry to larger audiences. The strings of both instruments were struck with a short stick, or plectrum.

The Muses, daughters of Zeus and Mnemosyne, were originally three in number and presided over song and dance. But their ranks were later increased to nine to include different branches of the arts and sciences: history, lyric poetry, epic poetry, comedy, tragedy, dance and song, love poetry, hymns, and astronomy.

c. 440 B.C. British Museum, London

FLUTE PLAYER

Training in music was part of every Greek schoolboy's education, and among the instruments in which pupils were expected to acquire proficiency was the *aulos,* or double flute, played with the aid of a mouth band to keep the two ends together at the lips. The flute was used in Greece on a wide variety of occasions —to accompany dancing and singing at banquets, to lead men into battle, to accompany athletic contests, and to keep marchers in step in processions. Greek philosophers criticized the flute: Aristotle said it aroused violent emotions instead of disciplining the soul, and Plato condemned it for its composite use of harmony. "Beauty of style, and harmony, and grace, and good rhythm," he said, "depend on simplicity."

The painter of this detail on a red-figure wine jar was one of the finest of Athenian vase painters of the early fifth century B.C. Known as the Kleophrades Painter, he was one of the most prolific artists of the red-figure technique: more than a hundred of his vases survive. The figure of the flute player has a powerful, almost three-dimensional solidity, and his vivid checkered tunic with tasseled hem adds life to the composition. The convention of earlier black-figure painting by which the eye was shown frontally even in a profile head has here given way to the more realistic profile view of red-figure art, with the pupil well forward in the eye.

490-480 B.C. British Museum, London

TEMPLE OF CONCORD
AT AGRIGENTUM

Sicily was a major goal of the wave of emigrating Greeks who, starting in the mid-eighth century B.C., sailed out from their homeland to found colonies around the Mediterranean. This so-called Temple of Concord was being raised at Acragas (the Roman Agrigentum) on the southern coast of Sicily at about the same time that the Parthenon was being built in Athens; it shares with it many of the classic features of the Doric order, though it is built of local limestone rather than the fine marble of the Parthenon.

Above the three tall steps rise the strong Doric columns, tapering upward toward their capitals. The architrave and frieze across the tops of the columns are still intact. Above is the pediment, formed from a projecting cornice enclosing a flat triangular gable, or tympanum. The pediment of the Greek temple was sometimes ornamented with sculpture, more or less in the round. In ancient times, moldings and sculptures would have been painted in bright colors that glowed in the Mediterranean sun.

Agrigentum, first colonized by the Greeks in about 580 B.C., soon became an important city, with temples to Zeus, Hera, Demeter, and Hephaestus. The Greeks in Sicily were frequently attacked by the Carthaginians, and Agrigentum itself was captured and devastated in about 406 B.C. The Temple of Concord survived the attack, and its good state of preservation through the centuries is largely due to the fact that it was later converted into a Christian church.

440 B.C.

THE ACROPOLIS

The high, rocky plateau of the Acropolis, which towers more than 300 feet above the modern city of Athens, was the birthplace of the original Athenian city-state. Most early Greek settlements were centered around a hilltop, which served as a natural defense against invaders. The steep-sided *acropolis*, or "high city," of Athens formed a well-nigh impregnable fortress.

With the revival of Greek civilization that began around 800 B.C., after the Dark Ages, the *polis*, or city-state, of Athens spread beyond the ancient walls. The Acropolis, where the city began, became a place of worship. The first of several temples was built on the Acropolis in about 600 B.C., but all these early shrines were destroyed when the Persians sacked Athens in 480 B.C. The fine marble buildings that crown the Acropolis today were created by Pericles and his successors during the "Golden Age" of Athens, following the expulsion of the Persian invaders.

The centerpiece of the Acropolis was the mighty Parthenon, soaring sixty-five feet into the sky on forty-six marble columns. On the northwest side of the Acropolis (at the left of the picture) stands a broad Propylaea, or monumental gateway, through whose five doors the citizens of Athens approached the holy places of the Acropolis after climbing from the town below. Two other buildings were erected during the last quarter of the fifth century: the temple of Athena Nike, just to the right of the Propylaea, and the Erechtheion, behind them both.

After Greece became part of the Roman Empire, Athens continued to flourish. The ruined walls below the Acropolis, visible through the trees in the foreground, are those of the Odeon, or public theater, built by the wealthy philanthropist Herodes Atticus during the rule of Marcus Aurelius in the second century A.D.

Fifth century B.C.

PERICLES, MASTER
OF GOLDEN-AGE ATHENS

"Our city is an education to Greece." This was the proud boast of the statesman Pericles, under whose influence from around 455 B.C. until his death in 429 B.C. the city of Athens enjoyed a Golden Age. This marble portrait of Pericles is a Roman copy of a bust made by the Athenian sculptor Cresilas during Pericles' lifetime. The sculptor has carved a face expressing a calm dignity and statesmanlike wisdom, conveying in stone some of the awe in which fellow Athenians held their leader.

Pericles wears a helmet, pushed back onto the top of his head, as a symbol of his role as *strategus*, one of the commanders of the city's forces—for it was as a military leader as well as a skilled orator that Pericles rose to prominence. He led the forces of Athens to victory over rival city-states, and with a series of victories at sea made the entire Aegean world an Athenian empire. Funds poured into the Athenian treasury from Greek states around the Aegean as a levy for mutual defenses against Persia. Pericles used this wealth to build up a great Athenian fleet, and also to finance an ambitious program of building works on the Acropolis, designed to embody in marble the self-confidence of Athens and to make it the wonder of the entire Greek world.

The time of Pericles was a time of achievement by Greeks in many fields. The Athenian theater reached its peak in the great tragic dramas of Aeschylus, Euripides, and Sophocles; Herodotus, with his account of the wars against Persia, created a work that earned him the title of "father of history"; and philosophers such as Anaxagoras, by applying the exercise of reason to the workings of the world around them, were laying the foundations of scientific inquiry.

c. 440 B.C. British Museum, London

THE PARTHENON

The Parthenon in Athens is the crowning glory of Classical architecture, expressing to perfection the Greek ideals of harmony and order. Rediscovered during the Renaissance, the Classical style has been one of the dominant influences on Western architecture for the last five hundred years, and the principal features of the Parthenon are reflected in the design of innumerable buildings throughout the Western world.

The Parthenon was built to the glory of Athena, the patron goddess of Athens, whose citizens believed she had played a major role in helping them to defeat the invading Persians. The heart of the temple was the actual shrine of Athena Parthenos, "Athena the Maiden," a rectangular building containing two separate chambers. One was a treasury in which offerings to the goddess were placed; in the adjoining room stood an imposing wooden statue of Athena.

The shrine of Athena was enclosed by a rectangular colonnade of simple, sturdy Doric columns. To give the eye the impression of perfect symmetry, the columns taper toward the top and are inclined very slightly inward. At 227 feet long and 101 feet wide, the temple was the largest in mainland Greece. The fine quality marble has weathered over the centuries to a golden honey color; in classical times the sculptured friezes and pediments were bright with red, gold, and blue paint.

Begun in 447 B.C., the Parthenon took ten years to build, and it was another six years before its decorations were completed. It remained a temple to Athena for another nine hundred years, and then became a Christian church and a Muslim mosque. In 1687, however, a Venetian shell touched off a Turkish gunpowder store within its walls, blowing off the roof and reducing many of the decorations to ruins. Today, corrosion both from the polluted Athenian air and from modern iron tie-bars inside the stone blocks poses a new threat to the outstanding monument of the city's Golden Age.

447-432 B.C.

102

DIONYSUS AT THE BIRTH OF ATHENA

Massive sculptures surmounting the broad eastern entrance to the Parthenon depicted the birth of Athena, the goddess to whom the temple was dedicated. Carved in the round like freestanding sculptures, these figures filled the pediment—the triangular gable that closed off the upper part of the temple, between the sloping roofs. The entire pediment stretched ninety feet from side to side, and the figures in the center of the group towered eleven feet high. Reclining figures are skillfully used to fill the diminishing space at the tapering ends of the pediment; this figure at the left end probably represents Dionysus, god of fertility and festivity and a son of Zeus. Even in its mutilated state, the figure exhibits many of the qualities of Greek figure sculpture at its height: the body in its relaxed pose is absolutely lifelike and anatomically accurate in every detail, and the realism of the scene is rounded off by the deeply carved folds of the drapery against which he lies.

The pediment was badly damaged when the Parthenon was converted into a Christian church in the fifth century A.D., and the subject of its central scene is known only from a description by the second-century A.D. Greek writer Pausanias. It showed Athena just having emerged fully grown from the head of Zeus, whose skull was split by the ax of the god Hephaestus to deliver the goddess.

438-432 B.C. British Museum, London

RIDERS OF THE

PANATHENAIC PROCESSION

Every fourth year the people of Athens took part in the Great Panathenaea, an elaborate festival in honor of their patron goddess, Athena. The procession at the climax of the festival was the subject of a continuous marble frieze which runs around the *cella*, or main chamber, of the Parthenon inside the colonnade. These youths on horseback are part of the long procession, which wound its way through the streets of Athens to an olive-wood statue of Athena on the Acropolis. The frieze is in low relief—only about two inches deep—yet the skilled carving vividly portrays the spirited mounts tossing their heads in impatience as their riders tug at the reins to keep them in line. Rivet holes in the horses' manes and mouths show where bronze reins and bridles were originally set.

Other parts of the 524-foot-long frieze show the remainder of the Panathenaic procession. There are cattle and sheep for sacrifice; girls carrying jugs to pour libations at the ceremony; boys carrying water jars and old men bearing olive branches; officials and musicians; and troops of mounted horsemen and charioteers. It has been suggested that the horsemen may represent the 192 Athenian soldiers who died resisting the Persian invaders at Marathon, and that in commemorating their feat on the Parthenon in this way, the people of Athens were according the victorious dead the semi-divine status of heroes.

Damaged by a gunpowder explosion in 1687, the frieze suffered further from the ravages of time. In 1812, surviving sections of it were taken to England by Lord Elgin, then British Ambassador to Constantinople, where they became part of the British Museum collection known to generations of visitors as the Elgin marbles.

c. 435 B.C. British Museum, London

SACRED ROBE OF ATHENA

At the climax of the quadrennial Great Panathenaea in ancient Athens, a new *peplos*, or woven robe, was presented to the olive-wood statue of the goddess Athena on the Acropolis. This scene, from the eastern section of the marble frieze around the Parthenon, shows a magistrate and his child assistant holding the folded garment, which was richly embroidered by the daughters of the leading families of Athens with scenes of the mythical Battle of Giants. The Giants were believed to be the offspring of the earth goddess Ge, who warred against the gods of Olympus. With Athena's special guidance and the help of Heracles and Dionysus, the gods vanquished the Giants.

Adjoining sections of the frieze show the gods themselves attending the presentation of the *peplos* to Athena. Before the ceremony, the sacred robe was borne through the streets of Athens in a long procession, which is represented on the remainder of the frieze. The procession set off at sunrise and marched through the streets of the city to the sound of flute music, with the *peplos* carried upon a wheeled ship. Near the Agora, the old marketplace near the foot of the Acropolis, the *peplos* was removed from its carriage and borne to the summit on foot. Part of the ceremony involved the sacrifice of a hundred oxen, a ritual which accompanied most religious festivals in ancient Greece. This hecatomb, or slaughter of a hundred beasts, gave its name to the month of Hekatombaion (spanning our July and August), during which the Great Panathenaea was held.

c. 440 B.C. British Museum, London

THE ERECHTHEION

On the north side of the Acropolis in Athens, close to the Parthenon, stands this smaller temple known as the Erechtheion. Whereas the Parthenon was built to the sole glory of the goddess Athena, the Erechtheion has four separate chambers, each serving as a shrine to a different cult. The Parthenon is distinguished by precise symmetry of design and the restrained grandeur of its Doric columns; the Erechtheion, on the other hand, is irregular in plan and much more ornate in style. It is built on different levels because of the slope of the hill on which it stands, its columns have the molded bases and scroll-like capitals of the Ionic order, and the roof of one porch is entirely supported by female statues.

The Erechtheion was believed to mark the spot where Poseidon, competing with Athena for control of Athens, struck the ground with his sea-god's trident to make a salt spring appear. Athena responded by planting an olive tree. The gods judged her gift the more useful to mortals and gave Athena the city, which henceforth bore her name. A statue of the goddess, carved in olive wood, stood in the easternmost chamber of the Erechtheion and was venerated in the Panathenaic festival. In case Poseidon should wish to repeat his beneficence, the Athenians left a hole in the roof of the Erechtheion.

The temple is named after Erechtheus, said by legend to have been an early ruler of Athens. Partly human and partly serpent in shape, he was also honored in the temple. The contest between Athena and Poseidon was believed to have taken place during the reign of the legendary Cecrops, the first king of Attica in wholly human shape. His supposed tomb was also within the Erechtheum.

421-406 B.C.

CARYATID FROM THE ERECHTHEION

This finely sculpted marble figure is one of six caryatids that supported the roof of the south porch, or Porch of the Maidens, of the Erechtheion on the Acropolis in Athens. Her *peplos*, or robe, clings close to the body, revealing its contours and showing the left foot held forward, as if to support the roof's weight. The use of female figures instead of columns is characteristic of the highly decorative pattern employed by the architect of the Erechtheion; the sculptor has arranged the statue's robe in folds that resemble the fluted Ionic columns used at the temple's other entrances.

The caryatid is named after the women of Caryae, a town of Laconia in southern Greece whose women were apparently famed as ideal figures of Greek womanhood. Caryae was the site of a temple to the goddess Artemis, whose annual festival included a ritual known as the dance of the Lacedaemonian virgins. The Roman writer on architecture Vitruvius believed that the use of these female figures to support the roof of the Erechtheion symbolized the enslavement of the Caryaean women by the Greeks in punishment for their disloyalty during the wars against the Persians.

This particular caryatid was taken from Athens to Britain by Lord Elgin in 1801-4 and replaced by a concrete copy. Today, because of the air pollution that threatens all the monuments of the Acropolis, the remaining figures face removal to the safety of an Athens museum.

c. 415 B.C. British Museum, London

112

TEMPLE OF ATHENA NIKE

The immense program of public-building works on the Acropolis, begun by Pericles after the Persian invaders were expelled from Greece, continued during the war with Sparta that broke out in 431 B.C. The small temple of Athena Nike on the southwestern tip of the Acropolis was designed by Callicrates, one of the architects of the Parthenon; but the main work of building is thought to have begun in 427 B.C. at the instigation of Nicias, a leading figure in Athens during the Peloponnesian War.

Like the Parthenon itself, this smaller temple is dedicated to the city's patron goddess, Athena—but here she was venerated in her special role as Nike, goddess of victory. Although most statues of Nike show her with wings, the cult statue in this new shrine showed her as *apteros*, or wingless. The Athenians may have wished to ensure that the goddess who had given them victory over Persia would not fly away and desert them in their new war against the Spartans.

Instead of the unadorned Doric columns of the Parthenon, Callicrates used here the more ornate Ionic columns with their decorative bases and scrolls at the capitals. There are four columns at each end of the central *cella*, or sanctuary, in which the cult statue of Athena was housed. The temple was dismantled in 1686 when a Turkish garrison on the Acropolis used it as a gun emplacement. Its present form is largely a reconstruction dating from the 1930s.

c. 427 B.C.

TEMPLE OF HEPHAESTUS

The architectural achievements of Athens in the time of Pericles were not limited to the great buildings upon the Acropolis. On a lower hill, overlooking the ancient *agora*, or marketplace, of Athens, stands this Temple of Hephaestus, the god of fire. Built in Doric style of the same Pentelic marble as the Parthenon, it was long used as a church, and as a consequence it is today the best preserved of all Greek Classical temples.

The Temple of Hephaestus is smaller than the Parthenon, with the more common number of thirteen columns along each side and six across the front and back instead of the Parthenon's seventeen and eight. The panels of the frieze over these outer columns are still in place. Within is the customary *cella*, or central chamber, with a porch at each end. The sculptured frieze over the front of these porches is also still intact.

Hephaestus, the son of Zeus and Hera, was especially revered by the Athenians because of his association with metalworking and, hence, with fine workmanship of all kinds. He was said to have made all the palaces of the gods and much of the weaponry and armor of the legendary Greek heroes. Homer describes how the armor and shield of Achilles were forged by Hephaestus in his bronze palace on Mount Olympus, where twenty pairs of bellows worked by magic at the god's bidding.

The temple is also called the Theseum, because it was once mistaken for a precinct of that name that is known to have stood near the site in ancient times.

c. *449-444* B.C.

RAPE OF THE LEUCIPPIDS

The mythical abduction of the daughters of Leucippus, a prince of Messenia in southern Greece, is depicted in this red-figure painting on an Attic water jar. According to the myth, the two girls, Phoibe and Hilaeira, were about to be married and invited their cousins, the twin heroes Castor and Pollux, to the wedding. When Castor and Pollux arrived, however, they seized the two girls and carried them home to Laconia as their own brides.

The riot of action is accommodated within the confines of the vase by setting the figures on different levels. At the upper left, one brother stands ready to drive one daughter away in his chariot. At the center, the second brother is guiding the other daughter, eyes downcast, back to his chariot. The abduction is said to have taken place in a sanctuary at which the two sisters were priestesses; the artist shows an altar in the lower part of the painting and, at the top, a cult statue of the goddess.

The vase is signed by a potter named Meidias, and so the artist who decorated it is known as the Meidias Painter. The highly decorative style is typical of Attic vase painting during the latter part of the fifth century B.C. The figures are delicately drawn, with many of the faces painted realistically in oblique view. Fine strokes in a diluted glaze depict the almost transparent draperies of the female figures; the effect of clinging drapery is similar to that achieved by sculptors of the same period by delicate carving in marble.

c. 410 B.C. British Museum, London

NEREID OR SEA NYMPH

This female figure, about four and a half feet high, is one of several that stood between the Ionic columns of an ornate tomb on a hill in Xanthos, a city in Asia Minor. It is thought to represent a Nereid, one of the fifty daughters of Nereus, who was believed to rule over the Aegean Sea from his palace on the seabed. The sculptor has represented the Nereid dancing over the tops of the waves, and the shape beneath her feet is taken to be a fish.

Xanthos, situated seven miles inland from the southern coast of Asia Minor, was the center of the region of Lycia. Greece had close trading links with Lycia, and Greek artists and scuptors flourished in Xanthos during the Classical period and adorned numerous buildings in and around the city. The so-called Nereid Monument was built for a local chieftain, in the form of a small temple, and the artistry of the sculptor who carved its decorations was clearly equal to that of his contemporaries in mainland Greece. The sea nymph's lively stance is emphasized by the deeply carved folds of her drapery, which, blown by the sea breeze, cling closely to the contours of her body.

c. 400 B.C. British Museum, London

FRIEZE ON THE NEREID MONUMENT

Settlements on the coast of Asia Minor were constantly menaced by the growing might of Persia, and the city of Xanthos was one of many that were sacked in the sixth century B.C. by Harpagus, one of the generals of Cyrus the Great. Though the city's fortunes revived in the following century, the designs of the four friezes which ran around the top of the Nereid Monument in Xanthos reflect the citizens' ever-present fear of Persian attack.

This panel, which is just over three feet high, shows a battle between Greeks and Persians; in this section of the frieze a barbarian on horseback aims a blow at a Greek, while a slain barbarian lies at their feet. By the convention of the time, the Greek foot soldier is shown nude. He holds a shield in his left hand, while his right hand probably held a bronze spear, now lost. The robes, caps, and battle axes borne by many of the barbarians in the frieze identify them as Persians.

Other friezes on the Nereid Monument showed scenes of battle around a besieged city, and scenes of bear hunting and boar hunting, which probably represent the pursuits of the tomb's owner. The tomb was destroyed, probably by an earthquake, and scattered slabs of the friezes were collected and taken to England in the 19th century. They have been pieced together in a reconstruction of the imposing facade of the monument, nearly thirty feet high, which stands in the British Museum in London.

c. 400 B.C. British Museum, London

ALEXANDER THE GREAT

History remembers Alexander the Great as one of the greatest generals and empire builders the world has known. In this bronze statuette, the young Alexander is clothed in the apparent simplicity of a goatskin cloak, such as a shepherd might wear. But the goatskin was actually a symbol of royalty to the Macedonians, a garment traditionally associated with Zeus and Athena, two of the foremost deities of Mount Olympus.

In a campaign lasting only eleven years, Alexander created an empire that stretched from Greece southward into Egypt and east as far as the Indus River. His career of conquest was initially fueled by the ambition of his father, Philip of Macedon, to unite the rival city-states of Greece and lead them in a war of vengeance against Persia, whose armies had invaded Greece and sacked Athens herself in 480 B.C. Philip was killed before he could realize his ambition, but Alexander achieved all that his father set out to do—and more. In 334 B.C. he crossed into Asia Minor to attack the Persian Empire, and within six years he had totally subjugated Greece's age-old enemy. Alexander pressed on to make all of western Asia part of the Greek world, and turned back only when his forces refused to accompany him further on a march that they thought was leading them to the world's end.

After Alexander died in Babylon in 323 B.C. at the age of 32, his generals divided his territories among themselves and established three great dynasties to rule them. The three centuries between Alexander's death and the rise of Rome into dominance are known as the Hellenistic age, for during this time the highly sophisticated culture of the Greeks, or "Hellenes," spread far and wide throughout the lands that the young Macedonian king had conquered.

Fourth century B.C. British Museum, London

ALEXANDER
AND HIS MOTHER OLYMPIAS

Alexander's rise as leader of the Macedonians owed much to the ruthless ambition of his mother Olympias, represented together with her son on this onyx cameo. Olympias was the third wife of Philip of Macedon and a princess of the royal house of Epirus. She exercised a strong influence on Alexander's upbringing, choosing for him such tutors as Leonidas, who trained the young prince in physical endurance, and Aristotle, who taught him the science of politics and government. Alexander's broad education gave him an enduring interest in exploration for its own sake, beyond the simple lust for conquest, and he always took scientists, chroniclers, and artists with him on his foreign campaigns.

Groomed to become king, Alexander saw the throne eluding his grasp when in 338 B.C. his father took a new wife and forced Olympias and Alexander into temporary exile. Philip apparently suspected—justly or unjustly—that Olympias and her son were plotting to seize his throne before he undertook his planned expedition against the Persians.

When the king was assassinated by a member of his own company of bodyguards, Alexander and his mother were widely suspected of inciting the murder. Olympias did nothing to allay this suspicion when she put a gold crown on the head of the corpse of her husband's assassin. Olympias was blamed, too, for the slaughter of Caranus, the infant son of Cleopatra, Philip's fourth wife; with the removal of this last potential rival to the throne, the supremacy of the twenty-year-old Alexander was assured.

Third century B.C. Kunsthistorisches Museum, Vienna

THE LION HUNT

The forced marches and pitched battles of Alexander the Great's Asian campaigns were relieved from time to time by elaborate diversions and entertainments that Alexander devised for himself and his Macedonian army. The regular troops held athletic contests and cavalry tournaments. For the officers, there were prolonged feasts, enhanced by freely flowing wine, and also the pleasures of hunting the wild beasts that roamed much of the countryside through which Alexander passed. This mosaic showing a lion hunt was found at Pella, the capital city of his native Macedonia. It is thought to depict Alexander, on the left, and Craterus, one of his most senior and trusted lieutenants, about to administer the death thrust to a lion at bay. The hunt may have taken place in 333 B.C. among the hills around Sidon, after Alexander had taken the city during his victorious advance down the eastern shore of the Mediterranean.

The scene is one of several mosaics at Pella composed of wave-worn pebbles of different sizes and colors, with strips of lead added to outline the figures. Such pebble mosaics were the earliest examples of a decorative art that flourished during subsequent Hellenistic and Roman times. The next step in the development of the craft came when pebbles were chipped into smaller pieces to allow finer detail for parts of the design. During the third century B.C., most mosaic artists began to use specially cut cubes of stone, baked clay, and glass in various colors; these permitted a much wider range of tones, and subtle effects, such as those achieved in the Issus mosaic at Pompeii.

c. 300 B.C. Archaeological Museum, Pella, Greece

THE BATTLE OF ISSUS

Alexander's victory over King Darius of Persia at Issus, dramatically depicted in this floor mosaic from Pompeii, was renowed as one of the great battles of the ancient world. For eighteen months the Macedonian armies, led by Alexander, had swept triumphantly through Asia Minor, making short work of the Persian levies sent by Darius to fight them. Then in 333 B.C., at Issus (on the border between present-day Turkey and Syria), Darius himself assembled a great force to challenge the young Macedonian ruler. But even the hosts of Persia's "Great King" were no match for the superbly wielded phalanxes of infantrymen and cavalry formations with which Alexander scattered the Persian forces.

The mosaic of Pompeii, based on a lost Greek painting, shows in vivid and colorful detail the climax of the battle of Issus, as the leaders of the rival armies meet face to face. Alexander, on the left, has brought down one of the Persian king's bodyguards with a well-aimed thrust of his long pike, and now charges on toward the ornamented chariot bearing Darius himself. Alexander sits astride Bucephalas, the stallion given to him as a boy which he rode into battle in all the major engagements of his Asian campaign.

Hero though Alexander was at Issus, the mosaic artist has depicted him not as a demigod but rather as a 23-year-old general, who betrays a trace of apprehension on his boyish features as he confronts the startled Darius. With Alexander's decisive victory, the Persian king was forced to flee the battlefield, where his forces were being routed. Darius lived to fight—and lose again—at Gaugamela before he was murdered by noblemen of his own empire, who turned against their king in face of the all-conquering Alexander.

c. 100 B.C. Museo Nazionale, Naples

◀ LIFT HERE

ALEXANDER: DESCENDANT OF HERACLES

Like other Macedonian rulers before him, Alexander the Great claimed descent from the legendary hero Heracles. This coin portrays Alexander wearing a headdress made from a lion's mane, recalling the hero's celebrated feat in killing the Nemean lion with his bare hands. According to legend, Heracles then donned the lion's skin to protect him in his subsequent labors.

Many of the needs of courage and skill performed by Alexander during his Asian campaigns bore the stamp of the Twelve Labors of his legendary ancestor. The young king led his Macedonian army for a total of 20,000 miles across terrain that varied from snowbound mountain ranges to sun-baked, arid deserts. No obstacle was allowed to slow their progress. To capture the port of Tyre, situated on an island half a mile off the Syrian coast, Alexander built a causeway out of stone torn from buildings on the mainland and cedarwood from the surrounding hills. The causeway survives today, strengthened and widened over the centuries by accretions of sand and silt. To cross the River Oxus, Alexander ordered his troops to make leather balloons stuffed with straw, on which they floated themselves across the water to meet the enemy. To capture a mountain stronghold near the Indian border, trained climbers scaled the sheer rock face using ropes and pitons like a modern Everest expedition. Elephants captured from the Persians were floated downstream on rafts, while boats used to ferry troops across a river were cut into sections and hauled overland by oxcart to the site of the next river crossing.

Alexander always went into battle at the head of his troops, surrounding himself with glory that earned him the epithet *aniketos*, "invincible." Through his achievements, the young warrior maintained his Heraclean stature in the eyes of the Roman generals who were later to conquer his huge domains.

Fourth century B.C. British Museum, London

TEMPLE OF APOLLO AT DELPHI

Dramatically set on a natural terrace on the lower slopes of Mount Parnassus are the partially reconstructed ruins of the Temple of Apollo at Delphi, one of the most sacred of all sites in Greece. Delphi was believed to be the true center of the world, the meeting place of two eagles dispatched by Zeus from the opposite ends of the universe. It was here that the god Apollo was said to have established the famous oracle, consulted by kings and commoners from all over the Mediterranean world through eight centuries. They came to Delphi for advice on all manner of subjects —ranging from when to commence the annual harvest to whether to go to war against another nation.

Apollo, the son of Zeus, was associated with wise counsel, tolerance, and moderation in all things; the precepts "Know thyself" and "Nothing in excess" were carved over the entrance to his temple. The oracle was held to be the true voice of Apollo, speaking through the Pythia, or sacred priestess, within the temple. Oracle seekers who made the pilgrimage to Delphi first underwent rituals of purification and presented offerings to the god. A goat was sacrificed at an altar outside the temple, after which pilgrims entered the temple and approached the *adyton*, or inner sanctum, where the priestess sat on a tripod. In answer to the supplicants' questions, the priestess was believed to interpret the will of the god through the vapor of a sacred spring in the lower part of the *adyton*, which only the priestess was allowed to enter.

The prophecies of the Pythia were interpreted by priests, but they often remained ambiguous. King Croesus of Lydia, told by the oracle that he would "destroy a great empire" if he went to war, promptly attacked his neighbor Persia—only to be decisively beaten and to realize that the empire he had destroyed was his own.

c. 350 B.C.

THOLOS AT DELPHI

Hallowed by generations of Greeks as the site of the sacred oracle of Apollo, Delphi also had a sanctuary dedicated to the goddess Athena. Though she was especially revered in Athens as the city-state's patron goddess, the cult of Athena as goddess of wisdom, forethought, and work had adherents throughout the Greek world.

The sanctuary of Athena at Delphi was set near the Temple of Apollo on the slopes of Mount Parnassus, but on a lower terrace. An unusual feature of the sanctuary is this circular building, or *tholos*. Circular buildings were uncommon in ancient Greece, where the traditional temple took the form of a central rectangular chamber enclosed by a larger rectangular colonnade. The Delphi *tholos* has a central circular chamber, but this is surrounded by a ring of Doric columns, their sturdy fluted stems rising straight from the platform below.

The exact function of the *tholos* is unknown, though it clearly formed an important part of the sanctuary of Athena and may have served as an additional shrine to the more conventional rectangular temple which stands beside it. Like most of the buildings at Dephi, the *tholos* was reduced to ruins during the Roman occupation, but it has been partially re-erected in modern times.

c. 370 B.C.

STATUE FROM THE MAUSOLEUM

This larger-than-life statue is one of the few relics of a building celebrated in antiquity as one of the Seven Wonders of the World: the Mausoleum at Halicarnassus. The Mausoleum was the tomb of Mausolus, a ruler of Caria in southwest Asia Minor. Though the coast of Caria was settled by Greek colonists, the district was ruled by princes of the native Carians, who owned allegiance to the king of neighboring Persia. Mausolus was king from 377 B.C. until his death in 353 B.C. He was succeeded by his sister Artemisia, whom he had married; the 180-foot-high Mausoleum that she commissioned as a memorial to the dead king was so widely famed that its name was later used to describe any monumental tomb.

The centerpiece of the Mausoleum is believed to have been a massive chariot drawn by four horses, carved in marble atop a tall stepped pyramid which in turn surmounted a temple-like colonnade of thirty-six Ionic columns. The Mausoleum had collapsed by the fifteenth century, but surviving parts of its sculptures were taken to England in 1864. These sculptures were on the same colossal scale as the chariot-group; this standing figure from the colonnade—reconstructed from more than seventy separate fragments—is nearly ten feet tall. It was originally believed to represent the ruler Mausolus himself, but is now thought more likely to represent another member of the ruling dynasty. The facial features and long hair are distinctively Asiatic. The identity of the sculptor is unknown, but the natural stance, firm features, and realistic, deeply carved folds of the cloak mark him as a Greek of the highest skill.

c. 350 B.C. British Museum, London

HEAD OF A BERBER

The gods of Mount Olympus and the heroes of mythology furnished the main subject matter for Greek sculpture; but sculptors of late Classical times began to depict in addition real people of their day. There are heads and complete statues in marble and bronze—so realistic that it is thought they must have been sculpted from the living models—of philosophers such as Epicurus and Socrates, statesmen such as Demosthenes, and numerous princes and rulers of wide areas of Asia and North Africa to which Greek culture had spread. There are portraits, too, of ordinary people in everyday scenes: a boxer resting after a fight, a drunken old woman, musicians and dancers, boys and old men, athletes and hunchbacks. Realism was extended to the portrayal of non-Greeks, including Persians and Africans. This bronze head of Cyrene in North Africa shows the head of a Berber, mustached and bearded; the features have an individuality about them that suggests the head is a portrait of a real person, whom his contemporaries would recognize from the sculptor's portrayal.

The Greek settlement of Cyrene, near the coast of present-day Libya, was founded in 632 B.C. by colonists from the Aegean island of Thera. That it became a settlement of importance is shown by the extensive ruins that have been excavated, including those of a large Temple of Apollo among which the Berber head was found. Cyrene was a major source of silphium, a plant so highly valued by the Greeks as a medicine and condiment that it became extinct in ancient times.

c. 350 B.C. British Museum, London

PERSEPHONE AND HADES

The deities associated with the underworld of the dead were represented in Greek art as recognizably human and benign figures. The couple shown in this south Italian vase painting are Hades and his wife Persephone, joint rulers of the lower world and of the souls of the dead. Hades sits enthroned, holding a scepter; Persephone holds a garland of corn.

According to myth, Hades, brother of Zeus, carried off the maiden Persephone from the upper world as she was gathering flowers. Her mother, the goddess Demeter, mourning the loss of her daughter, descended to earth and made it barren. So that the earth could bear crops again, Zeus sent his messenger Hermes into the lower world to fetch back Persephone. Hades released her, but only after a stratagem which ensured that she would spend part of each year with him in the lower world—the winter months.

The mythical Persephone probably symbolizes the seed, which germinates for part of the year in the earth before bringing forth its fruit. Wonderment at the earth as the source of all crops and minerals is also expressed in the alternative name of Pluto, "giver of wealth," which the Greeks gave to the ruler of the underworld.

Mid-fourth century B.C. British Museum, London

PERSEPHONE AND THE POMEGRANATE

This graceful terra-cotta statuette, only eleven inches high, embodies a fertility myth by which ancient Greeks attempted to explain the great mysteries of the growth, death, and regeneration of plant life through the changing seasons. It represents the goddess Persephone, consort of Hades and queen of the lower world, holding a pomegranate. According to the myth, Prsephone had been abducted by Hades from the upper world, where her grieving mother Demeter condemned the earth to barrenness. Hades agreed to release Persephone, but only after he had made her eat from a pomegranate. This bound Persephone to spend four months of every year with Hades in the underworld; her annual reunion with her mother on earth brought the seasons of fertility, when plants flourished and produced food for men's sustenance.

The statuette in terra cotta ("cooked earth"), originally painted in bright colors, was made as a votive offering to be placed in a sanctuary to the goddess. The style is known as Tanagra after a town in Boeotia where a large number of the figurines have been found. Similar figures were produced all over the Greek world during the Hellenistic period of 330-200 B.C. when the conquests of Alexander the Great spread Greek influence far and wide through Asia and Egypt.

Third century B.C. British Museum, London

THEATER AT SYRACUSE

Every major city in the Greek world has an open-air auditorium like this one at Syracuse in Sicily, where spectators sat to watch day-long performances of the works of the Greek playwrights. The origins of Greek drama are shrouded in obscurity, but one major influence appears to have been a tradition of religious festivals in honor of Dionysus, god of wine and fertility At first, these took the form of simple impromptu dances to a chanted accompaniment. Dialogue may have developed as one member of the chorus gradually took on the role of the principal character of the song. Around 500 B.C. Aeschylus is said to have added a second speaking character on stage with the chorus; third and fourth characters were later added, further reducing the importance of the chorus.

The central feature of every Greek theater was the *orchestra*, an open area of flattened earth some eighty feet across, where the chorus of the earliest festivals danced around an altar to Dionysus; the word *orchestra*, in fact, comes from the Greek word meaning "to dance." As the drama developed, a *proscenium*, or raised acting area, was built on columns to one side of the orchestra. Behind the proscenium a roofed building called a *skene* provided a backdrop to the action and dressing rooms for the actors.

In the earliest days, spectators sat on the grassy slope of the surrounding hillside to watch the plays. Later, tiers of seats, made first of wood and then of stone, were built in a semicircle around the orchestra, to hold as many as 20,000 spectators.

Third century B.C.

◀ LIFT HERE

MASK OF TRAGEDY

Performing in the open air, the actors of Greek drama are thought to have used devices to make their performances larger than life and to convey the mood and action of the drama to the furthermost corners of the auditorium. Prominent among these was a mask, made of linen stiffened with paste and molded to identify the character who wore it—comic or tragic, man or woman, child or adult.

Many of these masks were copied in more durable materials, such as bronze, marble, or terra cotta. This particular bronze tragedy mask, seventeen inches high, was found among the ruins of Piraeus, near a sanctuary dedicated to Dionysus, and was probably an actor's votive offering to the god. Festivals in honor of Dionysus were one of the sources from which Greek drama sprang. The word *tragedy* is thought to be derived from the Greek word for goat, which, as the enemy of the vine, was sacrificed at the Dionysiac festivals.

Other items of costume used by Greek actors to enhance the dramatic effect were high-soled shoes, long-sleeved robes, and body padding. The mouthpiece of the mask may have helped to project the actor's voice, though the acoustics of surviving Greek theaters such as those at Syracuse, Epidaurus, and Delphi are so good that a word spoken in the center of the orchestra can be heard all around the auditorium.

Fourth century B.C. National Museum, Athens

DEMETER, GODDESS OF AGRICULTURE

The bountiful goddess of agriculture and the fertile earth is represented as a woman of serene gaze and ample proportions in this statue from Cnidus, at the southwest tip of Asia Minor. The statue was found in 1858 at the foot of a lofty acropolis that formed the center of the Greek settlement at Cnidus. It was in a precinct dedicated jointly to the goddess Demeter and to her daughter, Persephone, goddess of the growing corn.

The statue, forty inches high, is in two parts. The head, of fine polished Parian marble, was made separately from the body and set into a socket between the shoulders. The remainder of the statue is of coarser marble, and weathering has worn away much of its surface. The cushioned throne on which Demeter sits originally had arms and a high back.

The calm features of the goddess and the deep folds of her clothing are typical of the style of Classical sculpture perfected a century earlier by Phidias and his contemporaries in the sculptures of the Parthenon. This particular statue has been attributed to the noted fourth-century B.C. sculptor Leochares, who was also responsible for many of the sculptures of the Mausoleum at nearby Helicarnassus.

340-330 B.C. British Museum, London

ALCMENE ON THE PYRE

The decline in exports of pottery from Athens after the Peloponnesian War gave an extra boost to the potters of southern Italy, who were the only real rivals of the Athenian craftsmen for good-quality ware. During the fourth century B.C., several different schools of Italian pottery developed, each with its own characteristic style. This ornate design, 6¼ inches high, is part of the decoration on a bell-shaped mixing bowl found at Poseidonia (the Latin Paestum) on the west coast of Italy. It bears the signature of its painter, Python.

The subject of the design is the sacrifice of Alcmene on a blazing pyre at the hands of her jealous husband Amphitryon, an episode from one of many lost plays by the Athenian tragic dramatist Euripedes. Alcmene sits on an altar, her right hand raised in appeal to Zeus (top left). Amphitryon, on the right, puts blazing torches to a pile of logs in front of the altar. The two female figures represent clouds pouring rain onto the fire; a rainbow frames the falling raindrops. The transparent, richly decorated draperies are typical of the style of southern Italian vases. Above and below are friezes of geometric patterns inherited from the Greek vases of four centuries earlier.

c. 350-325 B.C. British Museum, London

156

ADORNMENT

OF THE TEMPLE OF ARTEMIS

One of the Seven Wonders of the ancient world was the Temple of Artemis at Ephesus, on the west coast of Asia Minor. According to the Roman historian Pliny, the temple had 127 Ionic columns, each sixty feet high and "the gift of a king." This delicately carved marble group, six feet high, is part of one of the sculptured reliefs which, according to Pliny, decorated the bases of thirty-six of these columns.

The male figure, head held high, is Hermes, messenger of the gods and guide of the dead, identified by the *caduceus*, or staff, which he holds in his right hand. He escorts a female figure, who gathers her *himation*, or cloak, around her, while on the left Thanatos, the winged god of death, raises an arm, beckoning her to follow. The woman is thought to represent Alcestis, who offered to die in place of her husband Admetus, king of Thessaly, but was brought back from the underworld by Heracles; or she may be Iphigenia, whose father Agamemnon prepared to sacrifice her to appease the wrath of the goddess Artemis. The goddess saved Iphigenia by setting a hart in her place for sacrifice, and later made her a priestess of her cult.

The Temple of Artemis was built in the fourth century B.C. to a goddess whose cult was already established in the region before the Greeks arrived there. It replaced an earlier temple that had stood on the site for two hundred years before being destroyed by fire in 356 B.C., on the day that Alexander the Great was born. The new temple stood for six centuries before it was destroyed by the Goths in A.D. 263; after this, even the site was lost until 1869, when it was rediscovered after a six-year search.

c. 340 B.C.

CONVERSATION PIECE

The Hellenistic period, marked by the spread of Greek culture after the conquests of Alexander the Great, brought a growing interest among sculptors in everyday human objects. This miniature terra cotta, found at Myrina on the west coast of Asia Minor, is typical of numerous domestic scenes in the so-called Tanagra style, after the site in mainland Greece where the largest collection of such figurines was found. It is a charmingly lifelike study of two women sitting on a couch, engrossed in conversation; it has been suggested that the woman on the right is a matron advising a young bride on her forthcoming duties as a wife and mistress of a household. The bride holds a model of a hare in her left hand.

Both women wear a *chiton*, or long tunic, covered by a *himation*, or loose mantle. Although the group is only eight inches high, the features of the women and the folds of their clothing and of the couch on which they sit are modeled with absolute precision. The statuette was originally painted in bright colors, and traces of the pink of the bride's dress and the blue of the couch remain. Unlike the statuettes of deities, which served a votive purpose, these statuettes of domestic life seem to have been purely decorative.

Late second century B.C. British Museum, London

PIOMBINO APOLLO

The *kouros*, or standing male statue, of the Archaic period continued to be highly valued throughout Classical times and into the Hellenistic and Roman periods. The *kouros*, sculpted in marble or bronze, expressed the admiration which Greeks felt for the human physique; many *kouroi* were also intended to personify the god Apollo, and to stand in a sanctuary dedicated to the god. This particular bronze *kouros* appears to have been an attempt by Greek sculptors of the first century B.C. to pass off their own work as an Archaic statue of five centuries earlier, even to the extent of forging an Archaic inscription on one foot. The actual dating was established by a lead tablet inside the statue giving the names of two first-century sculptors, Menodotus of Tyre and [. . .] phon of Rhodes. The statue is usually known as the Piombino Apollo, after the site of its discovery off the Italian coast in 1832.

Apollo was associated with the sun, music, and healing; his principal sanctuary was at Delphi, site of the famous Oracle where the god delivered his prophecies through the mouth of a priestess. The Piombino Apollo probably held a bronze bow in his left hand as a symbol of his power to punish; in his right hand was a bowl for the offering of a libation.

First century B.C. Musée du Louvre, Paris

VENUS DE MILO

After being buried in the earth for more than 2,000 years, what is now the world's most famous statue was piled among other marble figures destined for burning in a limekiln when it was rescued in 1820 and taken to Paris. The statue, 6 feet 7 inches high, was carved by Alexandros of Antioch in the finest Parian marble, and represents the goddess Aphrodite in the form of a beautiful mortal woman. The familiar title of "Venus de Milo" comes from the names of the Roman goddess of love and beauty, Aphrodite's counterpart, and of the Aegean island of Melos, where the statue was found. The left arm once rested on a pillar rising from the plinth, while the right hand grasped the falling drapery.

Although the Venus de Milo is often thought of as typifying Greek sculpture, it was in fact not until well after Classical times that the female nude was portrayed in Greek sculpture. Until the fourth century B.C., while male gods and heroes had been depicted naked, women were shown clothed—albeit in clinging, semi-transparent draperies that revealed the contours of the body beneath. The dramatic innovation of the female nude deity came in 340 B.C., when the great Athenian sculptor Praxiteles carved a figure of Aphrodite laying aside her dress before bathing. The small, tilted head, broad hips, and long legs of the Venus de Milo derive from the example set by Praxiteles. But the vigorous sense of movement imparted by the jaggedly spiraling torso and legs reflects the taste of Hellenistic times, rather than the serenity and composure of the Classical age.

c. 150-100 B.C. Musée du Louvre, Paris

GODDESS FROM PERSIA

New deities were added to the Greek pantheon as the conquests of Alexander the Great brought vast areas of Asia under Greek domination, and they were still revered even after the new Greek kingdoms gave way to the even mightier power of Rome. The long-established cults of distant provinces were tolerated by their new rulers, and sculptors executed bronze and marble portraits of the objects of these cults in typically Greek style. This bronze head found at Satala —present-day Sadagh in eastern Turkey—is thought to represent Anahita, a goddess of Persian origin; but the features, the slight tilt of the head, and the brow encircled by a *stephane*, or headband, are reminiscent of many portrayals of the Greek goddess Aphrodite.

With the head of Anahita was found a bronze hand clutching a fragment of drapery, which suggests that the complete figure may have been modeled on a particular statue of Aphrodite bathing done in the fourth century B.C. That figure, the work of the Athenian sculptor Praxiteles, was the inspiration for many other sculptures, including the famous Venus de Milo. The so-called Hellenistic period, between the death of Alexander the Great and the ascendancy of Rome during the first century B.C., saw an enormous outpouring of statues to adorn the streets and sanctuaries of the new centers of Greek culture. Many of these statues were copies of famous earlier figures; indeed, it is only through copies made in Hellenistic and Roman times that many lost works of Greek Classical sculpture are known to us today.

Second or first century B.C. British Museum, London

166

Further Reading

Ashmole, Bernard and Nicholas Yalouris, *Olympia: The Sculptures of the Temple of Zeus.* Oxford: Phaidon Press Ltd., n.d.

Asimov, Isaac, *The Greeks: A Great Adventure.* Boston: Houghton Miffln Co., 1965.

Barron, John, *Greek Sculpture.* London: Studio Vista, 1965.

Boardman, John, *Athenian Black Figure Vases.* New York: Oxford University Press, 1975.

Boardman, John, *Athenian Red Figure Vases: The Archaic Period.* New York: Oxford University Press, 1979.

Boardman, John, *Greek Art.* New York: Oxford University Press, 1973.

Boardman, John, *Greek Sculpture: The Archaic Period.* New York: Oxford University Press, 1978.

Bowra, C. M., *Classical Greece.* New York: Time-Life Books, Inc., 1966.

Brilliant, Richard, *Arts of the Ancient Greeks.* New York: McGraw-Hill Book Co., 1973.

Bury, J. B. and Russell Meiggs, *History of Greece.* New York: St. Martin's Press, Inc., 1975.

Chamoux, François, *The Civilization of Greece.* London: Allen and Unwin, Ltd., 1965.

Christopolous, George A. and John C. Bastias, eds., *Prehistory and Protohistory to 1100 B.C. History of the Hellenic World Series: Volume 1*, Philip Sherrard, trans. Philadelphia: Pennsylvania State University Press, 1975.

Christopolous, George A. and John C. Bastias, eds., *The Archaic Period, 1100-479, B.C. History of the Hellenic World Series: Volume 2*, Philip Sherrard, trans. Philadelphia: Pennsylvania State University Press, 1975.

Cook, B. F., *Greek and Roman Art in the British Museum.* London: British Museum Publications Ltd., 1976.

Cook, R. M., *Greek Art.* London: Weidenfeld and Nicolson Ltd., 1972.

Coulton, J. J., *Ancient Greek Architects at Work: Problems of Structure and Design*. Ithaca: Cornell University Press, 1977.

Fox, Robin Lane, *Alexander the Great*. London: Allen Lane, 1973.

Finley, M. I., *The Ancient Greeks*. New York: Viking Press, Inc., 1964.

Graves, Robert, *The Greek Myths*. 2 vols. New York: Penguin Books, Inc., 1955.

Green, Peter, *Alexander the Great*. London: Weidenfeld and Nicolson Ltd., 1970.

Green, Peter, *The Parthenon*. New York: Newsweek, 1973.

Johnston, Alan, *The Emergence of Greece*. Oxford: Phaidon Press Ltd., 1976.

Kitto, H. D. F., *The Greeks*. New York: Penguin Books, Inc., 1950.

Lawrence, A. W., *Greek Architecture*. New York: Viking Press, Inc., 1975.

Mercer, Charles, *Alexander the Great*. New York: American Heritage Publishing Co., n.d.

Pope, Maurice, *The Ancient Greeks: How They Lived and Worked*. Chester Springs, Pennsylvania: Dufour Editions, Inc., 1976.

Quennell, Marjorie and C. H. B., *Everyday Things in Ancient Greece*. New York: G. P. Putnam's Sons, 1954.

Richter, Gisela M. A., *A Handbook of Greek Art: A Survey of the Visual Arts of Ancient Greece*. New York: E. P. Dutton, 1974.

Richter, Gisela M. A., *The Portraits of the Greeks*. Oxford: Phaidon Press Ltd., n.d.

Robertson, Martin, *A History of Greek Art*. Cambridge: Cambridge University Press, 1975.

Robertson, Martin and Alison Frantz, *The Parthenon Frieze*. Oxford: Phaidon Press Ltd., n.d.

Schweitzer, Bernhard, *Greek Geometric Art*. New York: Oxford University Press, 1971.

Tomlinson, R. A., *Greek Sanctuaries*. New York: St. Martin's Press, Inc., 1977.

Vermeule, E. T., *Greece in the Bronze Age*. Chicago: University of Chicago Press, 1964.

◀ LIFT HERE

ALEXANDER AS DEMIGOD

A portrait of Alexander far removed from the apprehensive countenance of the Issus mosaic is this stone head found at Alexandria. Here the young conqueror is portrayed with idealized features that recall Greece's earlier Classical age. The sculptor may well have been attempting to convey the awe in which Alexander's contemporaries held him as a man of almost godlike stature. The Macedonian rulers traced their descent from Heracles and thence from Zeus himself, and as Alexander swept across Asia in a storm of glory he encouraged his followers and the people of the territories he conquered to regard him, too, as a god.

A major step in Alexander's progress from mere man to demigod took place in Memphis in 332 B.C. After ousting the Persians from Egypt, Alexander was himself crowned pharaoh, heir to the throne occupied by the god-kings of Egypt for more than 2,000 years. It was in Egypt that Alexander created the great city of Alexandria— the first and greatest of many cities that he founded in conquered territories to immortalize his name. After the final defeat of Darius, Alexander adopted too the semi-divine character of Persia's "Great King"; and farther eastward he assumed the trappings and something of the tyrannical bearing of the Oriental despots he vanquished.

Fourth century B.C. British Museum, London

A KING OF THE EARLIEST GREEKS

The literature and art of ancient Greece are richly peopled with mighty kings and warriors of an earlier "heroic age." These heroes, such as Agamemnon, Ajax, and Odysseus, are idealized portraits of the artistocrats of Greece's prehistory—the leaders of a Bronze Age people known as the Mycenaeans, who flourished between 1500 and 1150 B.C. Four centuries were to pass before the stories of their achievements – heavily embellished by legend—were woven into epic cycles by bards such as Homer.

This mask of beaten gold was found in 1876 in a shaft grave, among the ruins of the hilltop citadel of Mycenae. It had been used to cover the face of a dead ruler, whose thin-lipped, majestic features typify the warlike character that enabled the Mycenaeans to dominate much of Greece. When the German archaeologist Heinrich Schliemann found this mask, he believed he was looking on the actual face of Agamemnon, the Greek leader at the time of the Trojan War, but in fact it dates from an earlier period of the Mycenaean age. The graves excavated by Schliemann contained, in addition to gold masks, a hoard of other treasures that provide striking evidence of the artistic skills of these earliest Greeks.

c. 1550-1500 B.C. National Museum, Athens